Change Your Thinking
Transform Your Life

———◆———

Practical Processes
for Renewing Your Mindset

Dr. A. L. Richardson, Sr.

Unless otherwise indicated, Scripture quotations are taken from the King James Version of the Bible.

Scripture quotations taken from the Amplified® Bible,
Copyright © 1954, 1958, 1962, 1964, 1965, 1987 by The Lockman Foundation. Used by permission. All rights reserved.

All Scripture quotations are taken from THE MESSAGE, copyright © 1993, 1994, 1995, 1996, 2000, 2001, 2002 by Eugene H. Peterson. Used by permission of NavPress. All rights reserved.

Published in the United States of America

Womack House Publishing, LLC
3965 East Brookstown Drive
Baton Rouge, LA 70805

info@womackhouse.com
(225) 356-1446

ISBN 978-0-9904219-3-1 (pbk)
LCCN 2016915403

For information about special discounts for bulk purchases contact Womack House Publishing, LLC.

Acknowledgments

I am so grateful to You Father God for your love, the obedience of Jesus and the indwelling of the Holy Spirit. All that I am and hope to be is because of You. I am humbled by Your grace.

To my dear wife of 40 years, Dr. Ava M. Richardson, I love you with my whole heart. I am so blessed to have you in my life. You are my greatest encourager and supporter. Your wisdom has been a safeguard and a place of peace and comfort for me. Your strength has been amazing. Your never-ending patience, admirable. You are a profound teacher of the Word and your dedication and consecration to the call of God on your life has been an inspiration to me. Your faithfulness is remarkable. I am a better man because of your belief and trust in me. I am forever grateful. I honor you and love you so much.

To our children, Adele, Trenell, Yarnell, Adam, Dannielle, Chris and David, I love you all and I am so appreciative for your understanding and patience.

My heart is my seven grandchildren. May this Truth and the ones the Holy Spirit will give to you impact your generation mightily!

To my daughter, Natasha, I love you and appreciate you with all my heart.

To the greatest church in the world, the *Christian Life Bible Church (CLBC)* family! Thank you for your support, encouragement and prayers.

To CLBC Team Book, who dedicated hours transposing this project, thank you for your tenacity!

To, Dr. E.L. Womack, thank you for believing in me and stretching me to do that which God has placed in my heart. Your encouragement is deeply appreciated. To the Womack Publishing Team, your dedication to compiling this project has been outstanding. May God bless you more and more and more!

Contents

Chapter 1

---◆---

Introduction to Change

If you were to ask someone what was the hardest thing they've ever done or had to deal with, you may hear such things as the loss of a love one, a divorce, losing weight, forgiving someone, and the list could go on and on. What if I were to tell you there is something even harder to do? Experts estimate that each person has more than 50,000 thoughts per day. As the Holy Spirit began to minister to me about the importance of renewing the mind, it became obvious that changing our thinking is one of the hardest things a person will ever have to do. What makes it even more difficult is the fact that we, as Christians, subconsciously don't feel the necessity to change our thinking. We all know that if we are unaware of what we are feeling or if we choose to believe that changing our minds is not important, we will not put the effort that is required to get the God results. However, when we do come to that place of understanding what we are thinking and feeling, we will learn things about ourselves. Then we will accept the challenge to enter into the mind renewal process which will promote change and growth.

Now we all need people in our lives who we seriously trust to tell us the truth. Why? Because the truth can hurt but it also can heal. You'll find it's not too bad to be hurt by the Truth. That's one of the reasons God's people gather in church each week—to hear Truth. Sometimes it's easy to embrace and other times it's not. Nevertheless, it brings deliverance, healing and soundness. But I know from experience that this temporary pain, if you press through, can result in permanent positive gain in your life.

God wants us to come into consciousness of the fact that we need to change the way we think. One important truth to understand is: we were created in God's image and after His likeness according to Genesis 1:26–27. In St. John 4:24, the Bible says, "God is a Spirit and they that worship Him must worship Him in spirit and in truth." Now if God is spirit and we(meaning mankind, the human race) were created in His image and after His likeness, then we are spirit beings.

> "And the very God of peace sanctify you wholly; and *I pray God* your whole spirit and soul and body be preserved blameless unto the coming of our Lord Jesus Christ." I Thessalonians 5:23 (KJV)

Man is a three part being: we are spirit beings who possess a soul and live in a body. When we were born again, only the spirit part of man was made new (recreated)—not our flesh, not our minds or our bodies. Only our spirits. To bring our minds in accord, into agreement with our spirits, Paul writes to the church in Rome, in our text scripture:

> "And do not be conformed to this world [any longer with its superficial values and customs], but be transformed and progressively changed [as you mature spiritually] by the renewing of your mind [focusing on godly values and ethical attitudes]" (Rom. 12:2a AMP).

If we have to renew our minds, then our minds were not born again when we received salvation through believing in Jesus' death, burial and resurrection. So, the thoughts and habits that we had before we were saved are still with us. The Apostle Paul wrote that it was necessary to change the way we think so we could live and enjoy this new life in Christ. By renewing the mind, the mind will be in agreement with the spirit. That is powerful!

We are children of God by faith in Jesus Christ. (Galatians 3:26 KJV). Now, as children, we must exchange our old way of thinking for God, our Father's way. A person could be battling generations of wrong thinking. Now, stop and think about that. Generations of wrong thoughts: that's a long time. To make it clearer: my Daddy received his thinking from his daddy and from his momma's daddy (his granddad); then they received it from somewhere, then they received it from somewhere, and now I have it. My point is: I had generations of thoughts to deal with. Now they weren't all bad; but, they weren't all good either. I am still renewing my mind.

Galatians 3:13(KJV) "Christ hath redeemed us from the curse of the law, being made a curse for us: for it is written, Cursed is every one that hangeth on a tree:"

Since Christ redeemed us from the curse, including every generational curse, you would think we would have no problems. But the reality is, we can be battling generations of bad thinking, so changing it is more than a simple notion. Changing our mindset will take work. It will also take discipline. I believe most of the problems we face arise from how we think: even after we have a new life, even after we are born again.

I'm not sure believers sense the urgency of renewing the mind. I'm not going to pretend like I'm free and clear because I'm not. I have to work this process every day of my life to stay free from the entangling bondage of sin. There are thoughts from my past that try to invade my life on many occasions. But when you know better, you can do better. But if you don't know better it's not even possible for you to attempt to do better.

Let's look carefully at our text scripture, Romans 12:1–2 again.

> I appeal to you therefore, brethren, *and* beg of you in view of [all] the mercies of God, to make a decisive dedication of your bodies [presenting all your members and faculties] as a living sacrifice, holy (devoted, consecrated) and well pleasing to God, which is your reasonable (rational, intelligent) service *and* spiritual worship.
> Do not be conformed to this world (this age), [fashioned after and adapted to its external, superficial customs], but be transformed (changed) by the [entire] renewal of your mind [by its new ideals and its new attitude], so that you may prove [for yourselves] what is the good and acceptable and perfect will of God, *even* the thing which is good and acceptable and perfect [in His sight for you]. (AMP)

There are some points I want to highlight. The first is that there is more to having a relationship with Father God than just becoming saved. Some people stop at getting saved, and don't continue to grow in their spiritual life. Being saved will allow you to go to heaven, but it doesn't *automatically* cause you to walk in the blessings that come from salvation in Christ.

Now I ask: "You've gotten saved, but where is it that you have stopped?" Is that as far as you have gone? If so, you shouldn't be satisfied with just being saved. God has a will for your life—a purpose and a destiny. Now if you have been satisfied with just getting saved, I challenge you to hear the heart of your Father saying there is more. Change your thinking and change it fast. Don't miss out another day!

Here's another question: Are you concerned about God's perfect will for your life? If you are concerned about it, He wants you to "get with it." Because He realizes we can't do it in our strength, He has given us the Holy Spirit to help us.

I want to fulfill the purpose of God for my life. I don't want to stand before God with a wasted life—never endeavoring to live out the will and purpose of God for my life. I hope you feel the same way.

Sadly, I have seen several people who don't want to pursue God's will because they don't want their "activities" interrupted. Yet, they were born with a God given purpose and that purpose is still calling to them. Many of them are doing a whole lot of things that they were not purposed to do. And, they are in hot pursuit of things that will never ever fit them. Therefore, I believe a good percentage of people are dissatisfied with their lives, even those who attend church. This is definitely not the Father's best. We must endeavor to make a change.

Nothing can fulfill the place God has in our lives, but God. The opposite sex cannot fulfill it for you. So, don't let a man keep you from your destiny in Christ. Don't let a woman keep you from your destiny in Christ. At the ripe, young age of 63, I am not about to let anything hang me up. I'm not about to put my confidence in anything on earth. All my confidence is with God, in Christ. When God says, "Time is up Pastor," I don't want to be worshipping something here; I want all of my worship to be solely Christ.

I heard an old preacher say, "Whatever you do for Christ will last; what you do for yourself (in a selfish manner), won't last." We all want satisfaction; but the day we stop pleasing ourselves, to please God is a new day.

Let's look at Romans 12:2 in the King James Version:

And be not conformed to this world: but be ye transformed by the renewing of your mind, that ye may prove what is that good, and acceptable, and perfect, will of God.

If God tells us "be not conformed to this world," then there is not an automatic disconnection from the world's way of doing and thinking. We must make a choice. Romans 12:2 (AMP) states,

"Do not be conformed to this world (this age), [fashioned after and adapted to its external, superficial customs], but be transformed (changed) by the [entire] renewal of your mind [by its new ideals and its new attitude]."

When people make the decision to follow Jesus and are saved, past habits and attitudes don't go away instantly. There may be some that seem to fade almost immediately, but there will also be habits and attitudes that will take time to be worked out with God.

God says you're a new man *inwardly*; your spirit is new, but there is nothing new about your mind and your body. The believer must actively work with the Holy Spirit in the transformation process.

The believer's spirit carries the will of God, all the time, in every situation and in every circumstance. However, the believer may be unaware that his spirit is loaded with this information because he hasn't developed spiritually enough to be sensitive to his spirit. In Galatians 5:25, the Apostle Paul wrote, "If we live in the Spirit, let us also walk in the Spirit."

Binding Habits

Even after a person becomes born again, old habits and attitudes hold on tight, like a pipe grip to their thought processes. The only way to be free of them, is to change one's thinking. Without a change in thinking, a person can never really be freed of those habits and attitudes. Without a mindset change, even believers, will display the same attitudes and same habits they did before they got saved. One cannot be freed from bad attitudes and bad habits just because they want to. Freedom only happens when a person's thoughts are changed towards those things—and the only way to change one's mind is to *renew* it. Anything worth having will cause for a change of thinking. Anything. If there is anything sinful that is still hanging around in our lives, it is only because we haven't fully renewed our minds in those areas.

Repetition is the mother of learning. Therefore, in an effort to build these truths within your heart, I will repeat them. Our text scripture, Romans 12:2 reads:

> And be not conformed to this world: but be ye transformed by the renewing of your mind, that ye may prove what is that good, and acceptable, and perfect, will of God. (KJV)

Some people tell me they know the will of God. But no one can know the will of God, until they have renewed their minds to the Word of God. Just because, I, as a Pastor, stand up and teach the congregation for an hour every week is not enough for true mind renewal. The difference maker is what a person does with the truth they receive—when they leave the church—what they do with it at home. It's what a person chooses to do with what they have learned that helps them really know God's will. Here's what most people yield to: They call the things they "want" to do, the will of God. A person can desire to do something so much until he fixes his mouth to say, "It's the will of God for me." That doesn't make it God's will for him anymore than it makes me an astronaut because I want to fly. That person may have missed God's will. But it doesn't make any sense to argue with him. Instead, patience and prayer must be applied.

Remember, change is hard. It is challenging. I believe that one of the problems here is that some of us must work more on being teachable. Let just say, for example, Sally comes to me and says, "It's the will of God for me to marry Bill." Now I know— and she knows—it's not the will of God for her to marry Bill. But if she wants to do it bad enough, she'll do everything in her power to *make* it God's will to marry Bill. Let me make an important point here: Binding thoughts and attitudes can be *dangerous*. Let's stop and think about that for a while.

Some things are totally out of character for God to do. For example, God wouldn't tell you to kill a person or to take another person's wife. Knowing God's character requires spiritual development which will help you to discern the will of God. Spiritual development doesn't happen immediately. It's a process. Don't let anybody fool you. It takes a relationship with Christ *and* consistent fellowship of the Word to develop spiritually. This doesn't happen overnight.

God's Word is His will. 1 John 5:14 (KJV) "And this is the confidence that we have in him, that, if we ask any thing according to his will, he heareth us:" To know God's will, you must become a Word person. And when you get in the Word, you will come to know the character of God. In Isaiah chapter 55, we can see that God's thoughts are higher than ours.

Isaiah 55:8–9 states,

> "For my thoughts are not your thoughts, neither are your ways my ways, saith the LORD. For as the heavens are higher than the earth, so are my ways higher than your ways, and my thoughts than your thoughts." (KJV)

Let's go to Proverbs 23:7:

> "For as he thinketh in his heart, so is he: eat and drink, saith he to thee; but his heart is not with thee." (KJV)

This verse makes it clear that a person is what they think. We also live the way we think. If we want to know how we think, let's take inventory of how we are living. If you want to find out if your thinking is right, again, look at how you live. Your living is a direct reflection of your thinking. Are there any areas of your living that you need changing? Then, change your thinking about it. Right thinking produces right living. Wrong thinking produces wrong living. Thus, how we think will be the key to how we live our lives and how we deal with relationships—including the relationship with Father God. The Holy Spirit showed me something. Your physical eyes only see what your mind thinks. For instance, I can say: 'there is a black dog over there." You begin to get a picture of a black dog. I can say: "it's a black dog with a bone in his mouth." You begin to get a picture with of a black dog with a bone in his mouth." So in reality, you don't see things with your eyes; as much as you see things with your thinking. The way you think is powerful! When a man thinking is changed, how he see things will change.

Once again, let's return to Romans 12:2:

> And be not conformed to this world: but be ye transformed by the renewing of your mind, that ye may prove what is that good, and acceptable, and perfect, will of God.

This verse implies if a person's thinking doesn't change, they will hold on to their old habits and attitudes, even though you are a new person in Christ. Our spirits become new, but in our thinking, we are the same old man. Joyce Meyers writes, "Whoever controls the mind controls the man." If you still have the same old thinking, then you are limited by those same old habits and attitudes.

No one can change their attitudes overnight, but they can start working on them. How? It's not easy, but it can be done…with help. Being conscious of the fact that one's thinking needs to change becomes the key to actually changing it.

Start with Following

How can you change the way you think? First, understand that God, your Father, has given you a Helper—the Holy Spirit. John 14:26 (AMP) states: "But the Comforter (Counselor, Helper, Intercessor, Advocate, Strengthener, Standby), the Holy Spirit, Whom the Father will send in My name [in My place, to represent Me and act on My behalf], He will teach you all things. And He will cause you to recall (will remind you of, bring to your remembrance) everything I have told you it." The process of changing your thinking starts with discipline. The word "discipline" comes from the word "disciple," which means "follower." So, we can say discipline starts with following. Consider cooking as an example. Being disciplined when cooking means following the instructions.

To be a disciple means to be a follower. A disciple of Christ is a follower of Christ. In my era of growing up, I was "made" to follow (but that didn't mean I was a follower). As soon as I was free, I followed nothing. Most of the time, I only did what I desired to do. Needless to say, the decision to do only what I wanted didn't work out good for me.

Following God's instructions will be a blessing to your life. Jeremiah 29:11 says, "For I know the thoughts that I think toward you, saith the LORD, thoughts of peace, and not of evil, to give you an expected end." In St. John 10:10, Jesus said, "I came that you may have life and have it more abundantly." God is a good Father and He wants only good for His children. He wants us to follow His instructions so we can live the good life He has prearranged for us. Let's look at scripture reference to confirm this truth.

> **2 Timothy 3:16 (AMP)** Every Scripture is God-breathed (given by His inspiration) and profitable for instruction, for reproof and conviction of sin, for correction of error and discipline in obedience, [and] for training in righteousness (in holy living, in conformity to God's will in thought, purpose, and action),

> **Ephesians 2:10 (AMP)** For we are God's [own] handiwork (His workmanship), [a] recreated in Christ Jesus, [born anew] that we may do those good works which God predestined (planned beforehand) for us [taking paths which He prepared ahead of time], that we should walk in them [living the good life which He prearranged and made ready for us to live].

The Value in Following

Have you ever tried telling a two-year old what to do? If they are unwilling, you will get resistance—maybe even in a tantrum on the floor. But when a parent let the child know that he is serious about him doing what is asked, following, given some time, normally the child will make a change. Then, there is joy in the camp!

Think about trying to lose weight. Losing a few pounds can be challenging. However, if you apply discipline your odds of losing the weight is far better. If you do not apply discipline, most likely you will not lose the weight. Why? Because discipline is a key to a successful life. When I first married Ava, years ago, I went from job to job to job. She never told me anything, but her attitude showed me how she felt. But do you know why I hopped jobs so often? I couldn't follow! I would start one job, quit it, and start another job. Thank God for a better understanding!

Learning how to follow is a big part of the process. And following anybody or anything—whether a manager or a recipe—involves discipline. If you can't discipline yourself then you won't be able to follow and follow well.

Let's look at one more example—husbands and wives. God has restored man to his Kingly position and woman to her Queenly position. They are to reign in life through Christ Jesus. Now the point I want to make is husbands typically like their wives to follow them; it's in a man's DNA to be a leader and desire respect. But, have you noticed that sometimes, as men, we are not good followers—that it is hard for us to follow? We are supposed to be examples to our wives, our families, of what "following" looks like.

When we follow the principles of God, we will become better leaders and receive the honor and respect that the Bible talks about.

What are believers to follow? We are to follow God's instructions. Let's look at Matthew 4:4 from two translations:

> **Matthew 4:4 (KJV)** But he answered and said, It is written, Man shall not live by bread alone, but by every word that proceedeth out of the mouth of God.

> **Matthew 4:4 The Message (MSG)** Jesus answered by quoting Deuteronomy: "It takes more than bread to stay alive. It takes a steady stream of words from God's mouth."

2 Timothy 3:16–17 (AMP) gives us the value of the Scriptures. I encourage you to take the time to meditate these scriptures and allow them to get into your heart.

16 Every Scripture is God-breathed (given by His inspiration) and profitable for instruction, for reproof and conviction of sin, for correction of error and discipline in obedience, [and] for training in righteousness (in holy living, in conformity to God's will in thought, purpose, and action),

17 So that the man of God may be complete and proficient, well fitted and thoroughly equipped for every good work.

When we follow the Word of God, we will grow. The Word is our spiritual food and guidance. When our diet consists of the Word of God, we will grow spiritually and we will have life and enjoy life the way God has preordained for us. Remember, He created us and has provided what we need, even before we got here. He is Omniscient and Omnipotent. He is a loving Father Who cares and have covenant to love us. While, we know there will be a challenge in changing how we think, in getting God's precepts in our hearts and minds; know that the blessing on the other side of obedience is far worth it! Embrace the Scriptures. Embrace God's ways and let's begin the journey now.

Notes

_____

_____

_____

_____

_____

_____

_____

_____

_____

_____

_____

Chapter 2

———◆———

The Challenge of Change

Again, changing your thinking is one of the hardest things you'll ever have to do, but if you will do it, it will spring you, as the follower of Christ, into a higher level of living that you will enjoy. As a spirit-filled, born again Christian, you have a *Helper*. Your helper is the Holy Spirit. Yes, He will nudge you to help you get started. The moment, you make up in your mind that you are going to start changing your thinking, and you start studying and meditating the Word, the Holy Spirit can now help you.

He will help you transform your thinking. I am personally living life on a higher level than I ever lived before. The love of Christ that's in my heart compels me to love at a deeper level. You can too. But here's the key: you have to "seriously want to." There is a big difference between saying, "I want to" and being passive about and saying it with a seriousness that you want to and you will do whatever it takes.

Creating the "Want To"

I want to open up something to you that perhaps will create within your spirit, your heart, the "want to." When I became born again, when I received Christ, I was really saved. I wanted to know more about Christ. I wanted to understand God's love for me. So, I surrounded myself with the Word of God which created a desire for more Truth and to please God. This is what happened to me. I'm not implying that I live a perfect life, but I have a better one than before—and I will be striving for perfection until Jesus comes.

I do thank God for a better life. The things on that lower level of living try to bombard my life, but I have changed my thinking and I know I can win every time! I boast in the Lord because this thing that has happened to me— the Lord has done it. Not only does He want to do this thing for me, but He wants to (and can) do it for you, too. Now I will tell you there are many different types of distractions that will come your way to keep you where you are. But you have to do spiritual things to create the "want to." Somehow when you get the "want to," there is absolutely nothing that will stop you. I Peter 2:2–3 (AMP)

> 2 Like newborn babies you should crave (thirst for, earnestly desire) the pure (unadulterated) spiritual milk, that by it you

may be nurtured *and* grow unto [completed] salvation,

³ Since you have [already] tasted the goodness *and* kindness of the Lord.

How do you create the desire for the Word? You taste it and taste it and taste it. You keep reading, studying and meditating and confessing the Word.

Proverbs 23:7 shows us that a person's life will follow the direction of their thinking:

For as he thinketh in his heart, so is he: Eat and drink, saith he to thee; but his heart is not with thee. (KJV)

This is a spiritual law which applies to everybody. Our lives go into the direction of how we are thinking. When we understand that law then we begin to understand that our thinking is very important. Let's go to 2 Corinthians 4:4:

In whom the god of this world hath blinded the minds of them which believe not, lest the light of the glorious gospel of Christ, who is the image of God, should shine unto them. (KJV)

The "god of this world" is a reference to the devil. Here the Scripture says satan blinds the mind—not the eye. This implies he is after our thoughts—our thinking. Why is the devil focusing on our thoughts, our thinking? Because our lives go into the direction of our thinking. Satan knows that if he can control our thinking and our thoughts, he can lead us anywhere he wants to. Now, that's serious.

But, I give glory to God because God knew this first and made provisions for us. He said to renew our minds to His Word. So, as we change our thinking, we can become more like God in our actions. Changed thinking equals a changed life!

Now let's think about what we think about. Generally, a person's thoughts may not be right or wrong. I believe our most dominant thoughts consist of what we like, what pleases us, what we enjoy and what brings us pleasure. When another person tries to disturb these dominant thoughts, we can become very protective and maybe even put those people in the "enemy' category. Because we think and maybe even say, "Who do they think they are? They can't tell me what I want, what to think, etc.?"

Pay attention for one week on what dominates your thoughts. Consider what you like, what pleases you, what you enjoy and what gives you satisfaction. If anybody disturbs that, how do you treat them? What are your thoughts about them?

Again , there is a challenge to changing. Who wants to change what they enjoy? Probably nobody! The fact that you enjoy something means you don't want to change it and that's the crossroad of wanting to change.

The Holy Spirit gives me vivid examples to help understand His Word and principles in His Word. So, let's look at a relationship as an example. In a relationship, most focus on what gives you pleasure, what gives you satisfaction, what they like about the person. Do you know that even as a believer, you can choose to ignore, not focus on some of the major issues that have been revealed such as anger, selfishness, etc.? We control what we think about. And, some make the choice of thinking only on the fact that the person makes them "feel good". If someone tries to get them to see how mean that person is to them, they can think that person is trying to take away what pleases them and that person just don't want them to be happy. This can be so far from the truth. But, it is what we think, that will determine our response. The fact that a healthy relationship should be centered on— Jesus—is often an afterthought. It is only when they mess up that they begin to cry out for Jesus' help, for His instructions. He's always been there, waiting for us to listen and follow His instructions. If our *dominant* thoughts are on what brings us pleasure and satisfaction, what we like, what we enjoy, we will miss the good life God has for us.

I drew this principle from something people are familiar with: cigarette smoking. Now on the cigarette pack, the surgeon general has made it known that cigarette smoking can be a hazard to your health. That warning is on every single pack on the shelves. But people don't pay attention to the warning on the pack. Sometimes people won't eat unless they have a cigarette! Even though they know how unhealthy cigarette smoking is, it doesn't move them to stop. Why? People enjoy the pleasure of smoking. It brings some type of satisfaction. The government warns that smokers are liable to die young; smoking will reduce a person's life expectancy, and smoking causes lung cancer, to name a few. But in some cases, that doesn't stop people! They ignore what is written. But ignoring it will bring consequences—maybe not for years, but they will come. Not only does it harm the person smoking but also second-hand smoke harms the ones they live with. My point is not to criticize people but to highlight that if we value something enough, we will totally ignore the warning signs even if it means our lives. Why? Because of the satisfaction and the pleasure it brings.

Pleasure is placed above everything, even health. Why do they only see one side of this and not the whole picture? Because if they looked at the whole picture, it would challenge them to stop doing something they enjoy. They know there are negative consequences, but they don't want to "think" about them. They are not ready to face the challenge. Therefore, they give truth a lower level of importance. They haven't yet put truth above what brings them satisfaction and pleasure.

Yet, the principle is still working and in this case, it is working against them.

We will only give Truth its proper place when we are in a serious relationship with Jesus Christ. People are in a relationship with Jesus, but the question is: to what degree? Are you serious about your relationship with Jesus where you are willing to sacrifice those things that give you satisfaction and pleasure if it is working against you?

Sometimes people are not ready for change. Again, they don't want to face the challenge. The Bible says sin is the strength of the law. This means the more somebody tries to stop someone or keep them from doing what gives them pleasure, the worst they become. Truth doesn't matter as much as the things that bring them pleasure and satisfaction. It is my prayer that since you are reading this book, that you are saying, "God I want to change, show me how." God's love is calling out to you to come to Him. The Holy Spirit will help you and your brothers and sisters in Christ will encourage you.

I found this challenge to be true where my life is concerned, until I grew serious about my relationship with Jesus Christ. Truth becomes more important now than anything else. But before a person has a real relationship with Jesus Christ, truth doesn't have its proper place. It doesn't matter how long and how often a person has been going to church. We must all make a choice to give truth it's proper place.

God's truth causes people's heart to change. Jesus says you shall know the truth and the "truth will set you free" (John 8:32 KJV). But people tell God, in a sense, to "Come back later" because they are enjoying life as it is right now and don't want to give this up no matter what message God gives. They are just not going to do it.

I have some good news: *God offers each person peace that no earthly, material thing or person can offer.*

Cigarettes and Changing Thoughts

Let's return to the example of cigarette smoking, which perfectly illustrates how hard it is to change thinking. Before I was saved, I was a smoker. When I was dating Ava, my wife, I would ask her to sneak me a cigarette. But on the day of my salvation, I stopped. How did I stop so quickly? Thinking. I had thoughts of pleasing God. Because I wanted to please God, I stopped. I used to smoke weed every day of my life. I had to have that little buzz when I was home after work, because I never wanted the buzz to leave me. I was high every day! I even rode a motorcycle while I was higher than a kite! I would wear dark glasses to hide my red eyes. One day I walked into the house and Ava was watching TV and I said, "I already messed up and now I'm about to mess up another life," thinking of my daughter. I said to Ava, "I'm going to stop smoking this weed." It was just in my mind that I had to have it every day. It's been almost forty years and I have not smoked any weed! I needed deliverance. I left that weed alone, but I set my mind to do it.

When some people are saved, they experience freedom progressively, but I was freed instantly. That freedom has allowed me to step into my destiny and fulfill my purpose. I'm walking in my purpose and my destiny right now—the destiny God had set out for me from when I was in my mother's womb. But I couldn't find it until I changed my thinking.

Though I had accepted Christ, I was still living in a lower level of life. Poverty was eating me alive even though I had been set free from the thing. A person can be set free from something through Jesus Christ, but thinking outside of the Word of God, will keep a person in bondage. I had to make myself think in line with the Word of God—and so does every believer. For me, that was hard. I was raised in poverty, and was about to bring my kids into that same life—until I got in the Word and changed my thinking. I learned that life doesn't breed luck. There is God's blessing or a curse. The only way to come out from under the curse is to be set free from it (Galatians 3:13–14)! But being set free from the curse does not mean a person won't still think about it. Because your life will go in the direction of your thinking.

Eliminate "Can't"

Believers must change their thinking—renew their minds. One word to eliminate from your vocabulary is "can't." Some people have marinated in the idea that they "can't." The Bible says those who believe in Jesus can "do all things through Him who gives [them] strength" (Phil. 4:13 NIV). Start at the beginning! For example, if a young lady's parents bought a $300,000 house, it doesn't mean she will be able to afford that same house—especially if her new husband isn't able to afford it. The principle: start at the beginning, and work toward goals. With God's help and grace, it will happen. The Holy Spirit will provide the needed support.

Everyone needs that little element of patience. Hebrews 3:36 (KJV) reads, "For ye have need of patience, that, after ye have done the will of God, ye might receive the promise."

The Bible says after a believer has done the will of God great patience and faith are needed, but the promise stands. So, it's no big deal to start small, but at least work the principle with what is available. That doesn't just apply to money. Start by eliminating the word "can't"!

It doesn't matter what the addiction may be—it could be a food addiction or a sexual addiction. Even self-satisfaction and the pleasure of this world can be an addiction. Even seeking fun can be an addiction, if fun is elevated before God. 2 Timothy 3:2–4 (KJV) reads:

> 2 For men shall be lovers of their own selves, covetous, boasters, proud, blasphemers, disobedient to parents, unthankful, unholy,
> 3 Without natural affection, trucebreakers, false accusers, incontinent, fierce, despisers of those that are good,
> 4 Traitors, heady, highminded, lovers of pleasures more than lovers of God;

This will be one of the signs of the last days. Why? A person's thinking impacts everything in his life! Not only does God know that but also the devil knows that. If the devil can get a person to think in directions opposite of God's ways, he knows the person will eventually begin to walk, to live, in that direction.

I could share with you testimony after testimony of how my wrong way of thinking got me in trouble and I mean big trouble. On one occasion, I was at a disco joint, as we called it back then. Some guys jumped me over a girl and beat me to the point I was bleeding. Oh, was I mad! I made it to my car to get my gun. But the hot tamale man ran up to me and said, "I see what you about to do; it's not worth it." I told him, "I got to do it!" He said, "you don't have to do it". And right then I can hear "you got to do it". Then the man said, "I know you have a future and you about to throw away your future." And I looked at him and the tears ran down my eyes. I said thank you sir and turned around and got in my car. If it wasn't for that man (and his persistent), I might be sitting in prison today, or dead. I had one thought— to kill those men—but thank God for one man. If I could see that man today, I would thank him.

If it had not been for the grace of God, I know I would not be here today. And, if I had not applied myself to the Word, if I had not renewed my mind, changed my thinking, I wouldn't be here and I wouldn't be enjoying life. It's one thing to be alive. It's another to be alive and to be enjoying life. Yet there are challenges every day. But, I have renewed my mind to Scriptures to know God really loves me and to know God really does have a plan and purpose for my life (Jeremiah 29:11). I have come to experience God's love and I am in a quest to learn every day the length, depth, width and height of His love for me. Changing your thinking can save your life and put you on the right path.

I am a living testimony that if you change your thinking; if you can get God's thoughts in your mind and heart, it will change your life! The Word of God has the power to do that. Take the "can't" out.

Notes

Chapter 3

The Mirror

People do not usually give up things of pleasure just because someone tells them they are wrong or "not right." Sometimes people think once they are saved and in Christ, they have to give up everything. I want to bring clarity to this. When I first came into the Lord, I gave up smoking and drinking, which were "obvious" things. I called those things "outward" things. But, then, there were some other things I needed to give up. These were what I call "heart" things. I held on to them tight. There were attitudes that I held on to that needed to change. I wasn't in love with those attitudes or made them my "god," but I knew that I wasn't getting any pleasure from the responses that my wife and children gave me when I exhibited certain attitudes.

At that point of my life, I couldn't see myself. The biggest blessing for anybody in life is to be able to see themselves. Sometimes it can take years before a person can truly discover themselves.

I want to show you something that should bless you. As I stated before, there are things that people get pleasure out of and enjoy doing that are not the best for them or inside of God's will. What will cause a person to surrender what he enjoys for God's will? Relationship. It is a genuine relationship with the Lord Jesus Christ. Countless numbers of people have come to Christ, but never developed a real relationship with Him through fellowship. A relationship with Christ is developed through fellowship with Him—spending time in His Word—coming to know, appreciate, and love Him. A person could be saved for forty or fifty years and still not have a true relationship with Jesus Christ. Having this relationship with Christ, through fellowship with Him, will motivate you to surrender those things that are not profitable for you and you will be glad to do it.

Once I had developed a relationship with Jesus Christ, through fellowshipping His Word, I no longer wanted to please myself. I wanted to please *Him*. When a person gets to the point where they desire to please Him, they will do whatever it takes to ensure that happens. Some will say pleasing God is not a profound revelation; but it is a truth that will bring liberation from all of those things that are taking God's place and attention. And, it will free you to live the good life God has promised you.

John 8:29 says:

> And he who sent me is with me: the Father
> has not left me alone; For I do always those
> things that pleases him. (KJV)

I must ask the question, even to believers: are you filled with thoughts of always pleasing God as Jesus was? Notice the scripture says Jesus "always" wanted to please the Father. This means Jesus had a true and very powerful relationship with his Father.

Sometimes I do those things that please God. But, the Bible says that Jesus *always* did those things, and we are commissioned to follow the example that Jesus set. Paul said in 1 Corinthians 11:1, "Follow my example, as I follow the example of Christ" (NIV).

Jesus did everything that He should have done to please his Father. Similarly, it is only through the relationship with Jesus Christ that I can give up the things that I enjoy and gives me pleasure. How can I enjoy something and have pleasure in it when it is wrong? Because knowing that something is wrong is not enough. People receive Jesus as their Savior all of the time, but do not grow and develop through their personal relationship and fellowship as they should. Therefore, the life God has promised is not manifested in their lives. It's a new day for you. Seek to know Gods' perfect will. Let the Word work in you and do what only it can do: change you inside out. Fellowship with Him in that relationship is paramount.

Have you ever had anyone in your life that you would do anything for—a wife, a husband, a girlfriend or boyfriend? Perhaps you became so close to that person that deep feelings developed and you would do just about anything for that person. This is the *fruit* of quality fellowship! When you come to know and understand how much He loves you, you are on your way.

We can only come to know our Father through intimate fellowship with Him—learning His ways, His will, and His purposes by spending time with Him through His Word. To know Jesus is to love Him. To love Him means seeking to please Him. When you want to please Him, nothing will stop you! Personal fellowship with Jesus, the Word, changes the way you think.

Think about spending a whole week with Jesus, talking with Him, walking with Him, even sharing meals with Him. Would your thinking change? Most definitely, unless you are rebellious.

Fellowship with Jesus causes something to actually change on the inside of you. It causes you to make changes that align with His vision and to be like Him in action. That is what He wants—all of us to be more like Him in all situations. The ultimate goal is to be like Jesus in character. Our Daddy wants our lives to reflect the image and likeness of Christ and that happens through *fellowship* with Christ—the Word.

Be Careful of Deception

There is a serious danger in enjoying and having pleasure in things that are wrong. Don't be deceived. As Christians, our hearts, our spirits, minister to us. Therefore, we should not want to be deceived in our thinking that we may enjoy things when we clearly understand that God does not approve. Remember, God loves us. Jesus came that we may have life and enjoy life to the fullest. (John 10:10 AMP).

Let's go back to the cigarette smoker. On the pack, it says that this product is a hazard to a person's health. It says smoking causes lung cancer, heart disease, emphysema, and may complicate pregnancies. With all that being said, smokers say smoking gives them pleasure and they enjoy it. Can a person *seriously* enjoy something that may be robbing him of a good long life, that may be killing him? If so, I believe this is deceptive thinking.

Wrong thinking is dangerous. Wrong thinking can be detrimental. Let's look at I Corinthians 6:19:

> Do you not know that your bodies are temples of the Holy Spirit, who is in you, whom you have received from God? (KJV)

Do you know that people refuse to smoke a cigarette in the physical church building? However, they will smoke and damage their own bodies, which Paul calls the "temple of the Holy Spirit." This can be hard to hear. But, remember, we must have courage to *face* the challenge and not run away from it, if we are to live as conquerors. While I'm giving the example of cigarette smoking, any other issue can be named here as well.

People want God to take away their problems and change all of their situations. While the Father cares deeply about our problems and situations, He is more interested in changing us. He knows if He can change us, through the process of mind renewal, then we will win over the problems.

Our thinking gives birth to attitudes. A changed life comes by changed thinking. Again, we are to exchange our thoughts for God's thoughts which can be found in His Word—the Holy Bible. Earlier in my walk in Christ, I realized I was listening to everything and everybody except the Word of God, including listening to my own thoughts. When I made a decision to change and started listening more to God's Word, it revolutionized my life. When I embedded His Word into my consciousness, my whole life changed. I was a better man, husband and father.

Christians win by pleasing Jesus. You will never lose. We need to understand that we are walking in deception when we think we need to hold on to those things we enjoy and have pleasure in that are outside the will of God. Everything outside of the will of God works death because it cannot possibly work life. Jesus came to redeem us from spiritual death, which would include deception. He came to give us life! So surely God doesn't want us into things that are contrary to His purpose. True life, the God-kind of life, is only in one source, and that is God. God is the Author of life, and everything out of the will of God is embedded into the will and intentions of God's enemy—satan. You remember, satan got kicked out of heaven because of how he thought! He wanted to be God. God said no way buddy! You've got to go! The end result of the things that are outside of God is death. They seem enjoyable, but they are working death in people. If you have a relationship and you practice things that are outside of the relationship, it is not working life. It is working death.

Here is what I want, and I believe you may want the same thing. I want the truth—the whole truth. I do not want to be deceived. Why? Because if we are deceived, we are unable to make good, quality decisions. We should welcome and embrace the truth, even if it hurts.

Everything that seems good is not always the best for you. I love bread pudding and it is so good *to* me. But, it is not good *for* me—it is full of sugar!

A person's thinking will never change until they are willing to grow and change. Parents must also come to that conclusion. No matter how we teach our children what is right, they are the only ones who can make the ultimate decision to follow.

Now that you are in Christ, you are not ignoring God anymore. You made the right choice. So, continue making those right choices. In 1 Thessalonian s 2:13, the people heard the Word of God, but when they heard it, they did not receive it as it were the words of men, they received it as the Word of God as it was in truth. We should receive the Word as the Word of God, the Word of Truth also. Not just words from men. Ephesians, chapter 4, reveals that God anointed men to preach His Word, not their words. Yes, they are imperfect; but the Holy Spirit in you, will bear witness to the Truth. Therefore, we should set ourselves to hear and study the Truth of God on a continual basis.

People who choose to do whatever they want to, do not have a free life.

Let's look at Romans 6:21–2 in The Message version:

> **20-21** As long as you did what you felt like doing, ignoring God, you didn't have to bother with right thinking or right living, or right *anything* for that matter. But do you call that a free life? What did you get out of it? Nothing you're proud of now. Where did it get you? A dead end.
> **22-23** But now that you've found you don't have to listen to sin tell you what to do, and

have discovered the delight of listening to God telling you, what a surprise! A whole, healed, put-together life right now, with more and more of life on the way! Work hard for sin your whole life and your pension is death. But God's gift is *real life*, eternal life, delivered by Jesus, our Master.

These scriptures describe the power of choice. We can choose to live our way or choose to live God's way!

If we allow our feelings and emotions to govern our lives, we will forfeit the real life the Scriptures outline here. In Matthew 16:24–25 (AMP), we read

> Then Jesus said to His disciples, "If anyone wishes to follow Me [as My disciple], he must deny himself [set aside selfish interests], and take up his cross [expressing a willingness to endure whatever may come] and follow Me [believing in Me, conforming to My example in living and, if need be, suffering or perhaps dying because of faith in Me]. For whoever wishes to save his life [in this world] will [eventually] lose it [through death], but whoever loses his life [in this world] for My sake will find it [that is, life with Me for all eternity].

Believers already have eternal life. But, it doesn't mean that we automatically live in it. Even though believers have eternal life, they must give up one life to live the other. Christians cannot live the abundant life as long they are holding on to the old, fleshly life. It is impossible to reach for something and still hold on to the things that are preventing you from having it. You must let go! Living the abundant life requires discipline. Do not become hesitant to move into this lifestyle because it is better than anything in the old life.

In the book of Galatians, Paul speaks about the works of the flesh:

> Now the works of the flesh are manifest, which are these; Adultery, fornication, uncleanness, lasciviousness, Idolatry, witchcraft, hatred, variance, emulations, wrath, strife, seditions, heresies, Envyings, murders, drunkenness, revellings, and such like: of the which I tell you before, as I have also told you in time past, that they which do such things shall not inherit the kingdom of God.
>
> ~ Galatians 5:19–21 KJV

Paul lists such things as adultery, fornication, envy, drunkenness and strife as things that are ungodly; those who participate in those things will not "inherit the kingdom of God," or the abundant life!

Those who walk in the spirit, however, will *not* fulfill the lust of the flesh. This process requires a change in thinking. Christians are so blessed, and God wants us to know it! There are untapped precious things, such as peace, that are available to those who seek the abundant life! There is nothing but love in the higher level.

Notes

_____

_____

_____

_____

_____

_____

_____

_____

_____

_____

_____

_____

Chapter 4

———◆———

From Relationship to Discipleship

A relationship with the Lord Jesus, which consist of personal fellowship with Him, will actually change the way you think almost instantly. Now we all understand that you can have a relationship with a person while not having fellowship with them. For instance, you may have a brother or sister, but you don't fellowship with him or her. We can have a relationship with Christ through the new birth, but it does not mean there is a "personal" relationship with Him. We have to be intentional about fellowship. Fellowship with the Lord Jesus will change your thinking. It is the missing element in the Christian's life. Fellowship with the Word.

Again, let's say Jesus came in the flesh, to your house and spent a week with you. Is it possible to spend one week with Jesus and not change? Would a week of personal fellowship with Jesus change the way the you think? What if it was just one full day? Would that change how you think? I believe it would.

> In the beginning was the Word, and the Word
> was with God, and the Word was God.
> And the Word was made flesh, and dwelt
> among us, (and we beheld his glory, the glory
> as of the only begotten of the Father,) full of
> grace and truth. John 1:1;14 KJV

Jesus was and is the Word that became flesh. We must come to the reality that Jesus and the Word are one. This Truth must resonate in our hearts. Is there any difference now between Jesus and the Word? Absolutely not! So, if you seriously wanted to have good fellowship with Jesus, all you have to do is spend time in the Word. Spending time in the Word is spending time with Jesus. It is possible to spend time with Jesus! It's as simple as opening the pages of the Bible and beginning to read about Him. As a result of spending quality time in the Word, the way you think will be changed. That's the power in the Word. It is the same as spending time with Jesus in person. We can do it every day!

The Law of Consistency

I remember reading about the "The Principle of Five". Here's a synopsis of it: Say there's a big tree that needs to be chopped down. Let's say a person approaches that tree and gives it only five chops a day. Five chops today, five chops tomorrow and so on. That tree will obviously not fall on the first day with only five chops! But it will eventually fall!

One of the problems people have is that they want to try to cut the tree down by making six hundred chops in one day. But the next day, they don't return because they have worn themselves out trying to do it all in one day. Most people who work like that never develop consistency. It's not the big splash that gets the job done—it's the constant drip. It's working "The Law of Consistency." Working a task out a bit every day and not rushing to put one thousand chops on it in one day, is far more effective than trying to get a huge job finished all at once. Think of building a house. If the house is constructed bit by bit, a little bit at a time, eventually it becomes fully constructed and ready to live in. That's the Law of Consistency. If you work on something a little at a time and be consistent, it will result in completion. To renew, to change your mind, will take consistency.

Knowledge and understanding of the Word are good, but in itself it doesn't provide the capacity to deny self. **It is our personal fellowship with the Lord Jesus which gives us the capacity to deny self.**

Knowledge and understanding must be connected with fellowship. You have to come to a point where you make your relationship with Jesus, quality—where you get to know Jesus on personal basis. When you do that, you will come to a point where you want to please Him in everything you do.

It's not possible to please Him and yourself (with the unrenewed mind) at the same time. A key to pleasing Him is to fellowship with Him. Believers don't often realize how much of a desire and passion they still have to please themselves. We may have some idea but we don't clearly know how much desire we have to please ourselves. As we fellowship with Jesus, it will be revealed to us how selfish we may be and as we yield to the Holy Spirit, we will come to a point where we want to please Him more. There are benefits and rewards that come with pleasing God and each of us can enjoy them now.

Priorities

A question I had to ask myself was, "Is Jesus first on my list of priorities?" Some people may say family is first; but, family won't benefit the way they could without having a relationship with Jesus. Everything we give to Christ, spills over everywhere else. I'm a better husband to my wife because Jesus is Lord over my life. I am a better father to my children because Jesus is Lord over my life. As we become people of the Word, our lives will emanate Christ! So fight through the drama of self; pleasing Jesus involves doing things His way and not our own. Jesus taught this, in Matthew 16:24:

Then Jesus said to His disciples, If anyone desires to be My disciple, let him deny himself [disregard, lose sight of, and forget himself and his own interests] and take up his cross and follow Me [cleave steadfastly to Me, conform wholly to My example in living and, if need be, in dying, also]."

~ Matthew 16:24 AMP

In this scripture, Jesus is saying if we desire to be His disciple, it will take self-discipline. The word "discipline" is like the word "submission." Some people don't like the word submission because they believe submission represents bondage and legalism. They also have the same feelings about the word "discipline". Self-discipline isn't easy, but it can be accomplished.

According to Matthew 16:24 above, discipline isn't bondage or legalism. It's rewarding and everything about self-discipline is positive. There aren't any negatives. If you have any negative thoughts about self-discipline, let's get rid of those thoughts today.

Notice in verse 24 Jesus said to his disciples, "If anyone desires to be My disciple, let him deny himself." Recall that the word "disciple" and "discipline" both come from a root word meaning "pupil" which means student. Therefore, a disciple is a student. As a disciple of Jesus, would you say you are a student of God's Word and God's ways? We must ask ourselves this from time to time. Remember, a disciple is someone who is submitted to the teaching of a teacher—one who obtains the thoughts and understanding of his teacher. Of course, we know that the Holy Spirit is our Teacher and He teaches the men and women of God what to teach us. So our submission is unto God and His order and government.

Self-discipline is the key element to establishing the order and government of God in our lives. Without the establishment of the order and government of God, people do as they please. The order and government of God over a person's life is what gives Jesus complete Lordship. When He has complete Lordship, He is the driver and we are the passengers. Some people don't even realize they are driving. Therefore, they are living life outside of the order and government of God. Jesus is Savior, but He must be accepted and allowed to be Lord.

Jesus being Lord isn't automatic. He can be your Savior; but it's how you yield to the order and government of God that will allow Him to be Lord. Yielding is still relevant today. As much as Jesus wants to be Lord, He will not bulldoze Himself into Lordship. How is His Lordship established? By yielding to the order and government of God. This involves self-discipline. Self-discipline is the vehicle that causes the order and government of God to be established in your life. Have you ever watched the Olympics and you see the participants train, how they deny themselves certain foods and pleasures, how they discipline their bodies, to reach for the gold? Hear me today, God wants us to discipline ourselves and receive His gold package—life, health, prosperity, peace, wholeness and so much more.

> Then Jesus said to His disciples, If anyone desires to be My disciple, let him deny himself [disregard, lose sight of, and forget himself and his own interests] and take up his cross and follow Me [cleave steadfastly to Me, conform wholly to My example in living and, if need be, in dying, also].
>
> ~ Matthew 16:24 AMP

Jesus requires the same from us now. In Matthew 16:24, Jesus said if anyone desires to be His disciple he must deny himself. Why is Jesus giving the disciples such a directive? Jesus lost disciples because of His preaching. If Jesus could be here today and stand up and say firsthand what I'm writing about, would believers still follow Him? Why is He emphasizing this thing about us denying ourselves? When we deny ourselves, our way, then God's ways (order and government) can be established our lives. The Lordship of Jesus can be established in our lives. Remember, Jesus denied Himself so that the will and purposes of God could be done in His life.

Life changing messages can challenge you to make adjustments. A call for an adjustment can be heard, but only when that adjustment is made will the glory and power of God work in your life. When Jesus is in the driver seat of our lives and we are the passengers, Jesus is free to take us in the direction of purpose and destiny. Jesus isn't free to take a life in the way of purpose and destiny on the basis of being saved alone. He is free to take a life in the way of destiny and purpose because He is Lord of that person's life. What does this mean? It means Jesus is the driver and the believer is the passenger.

In Matthew 16:24 Jesus speaks of self-discipline. There is no way around this if the believer wants to follow Him. He is also telling people to put to death any and everything that doesn't line up with His way. That's why He says, "Take your cross and follow me." What the cross represents is death—death to our way of doing and being right. He says to take up the cross and follow Him, because when anything comes up that's not in line with His way of doing and being right, we can put it to death. It needs to be crucified.

The "cross" here includes putting to death thoughts, imaginations, and reason that exalts itself against God's will. When Jesus says "take up your cross and follow me," He is saying there are things that will pop up through your thoughts and imaginations that will exalt themselves against His way of doing right. See, everyone that follows Jesus has a cross. Everyone has things, thoughts, and imaginations that go against His way of doing right. Christians are not exempt from this.

> For whoever is bent on saving his [temporal] life [his comfort and security here] shall lose it [eternal life]; and whoever loses his life [his comfort and security here] for My sake shall find it [life everlasting].
>
> ~ Matthew 16:25 AMP

Every man that comes to Christ receives eternal life. Eternal life is the life and nature of God. It is the same life God spoke about in John 10:10b where Jesus says, "I am come that they might have life, and that they might have it more abundantly" (KJV). Eternal life includes life as God would have for us which is an abundant and overflowing life. Here's the key: self-discipline is the *gateway* to unlocking the abundant and overflowing life. Jesus paid a price for everyone to experience this life and the promises that go with it! Everything He purchased belongs to us—those who love Him. But, to have a manifestation in our lives, we must first establish a life of self-discipline.

Christ did it all, but, we must have some form of discipline to walk in what He purchased. Christ said, "Don't use your freedom to satisfy your flesh!" What people call "free" isn't free at all; freedom in Christ came with a steep price.

People who do anything they want, anytime they want, lack a real sense of commitment. Commitment breeds freedom; but believers can't follow Jesus without having their "cross" with them. Thoughts must be nailed to this cross, as well as imaginations, arguments, theories, reason, and proud things that exalt themselves against the true knowledge of God.

When a Christian was born again, his spirit was recreated. Self-discipline is a part of our recreated spirit-man.

The Bible proves this! Paul writes in 2 Timothy 1:7:

> For the Spirit God gave us does not make us timid, but gives us power, love and self-discipline.
>
> ~ 2 Timothy 1:7 NIV

It's a package deal. God gave believers the spirit of self-discipline. He did it in the new birth. He did it because He knew we would need the ability to discipline ourselves. With the Holy Spirit's help, He knew we could follow His Word.

> . . . gentleness and self-control. Against such things there is no law.
>
> ~ Galatians 5:23 NIV

Paul, writing to the Galatian church, lists these virtues of the recreated spirit-man. Self-control is a part of the recreated spirit-man. When is self-discipline established? Self-discipline is established in everyday life.

Again, self-discipline isn't bondage, nor is it legalism. On the contrary, it's a part of the recreated spirit. Self-discipline is established by seeing the value of a thing. We can possess knowledge or some understanding of a thing but that doesn't mean we see the real *value* of it. A revelation of the value of a thing is necessary before we will honor and incorporate it in life. There is a difference between respecting something or someone and giving honor to it or the person. It is important to discern the two? King Solomon, who wrote most of the book of Proverbs, writes of this principle:

> "Where there is no vision [no redemptive revelation of God], the people perish; but he who keeps the law [of God, which includes that of man]—blessed (happy, fortunate, and enviable) is he.
>
> ~ Proverbs 29:18 AMP

> Where there is no revelation, people cast off restraint; but blessed is the one who heeds wisdom's instruction.
>
> ~ Proverbs 29:1 NIV

Where there is no revelation there is no self-control, self-discipline, or revelation of the value of a thing. I may have knowledge or understanding about it, but place no value on it. Where there's no understanding of the value, there's no self-discipline. A revelation of the value of being in Christ is vital, because in Christ everything changes.

Discipleship

Let's read Matthew 16:24–25 (AMP) again:

> Then Jesus said to His disciples, "If anyone wishes to follow Me [as My disciple], he must deny himself [set aside selfish interests], and take up his cross [expressing a willingness to endure whatever may come] and follow Me [believing in Me, conforming to My example in living and, if need be, suffering or perhaps dying because of faith in Me]. For whoever wishes to save his life [in this world] will [eventually] lose it [through death], but whoever loses his life [in this world] for My sake will find it [that is, life with Me for all eternity].

In Matthew 16, Jesus was talking about a time to come and that time is now. Self-denial has become a taboo word in the body of Christ. But to become a true disciple of Christ, the Scripture plainly tells us, we must deny ourselves, set aside own interests and pursue the life of God. It is time for the body of Christ to arise and be a light to a lost and dying world. To have the higher life, we must give up the lower life.

Then, in verse 25, Jesus reveals the reward for the man or woman who practices self-discipline. We will find life (life with Him for all eternity).

Let's go to 2 Timothy 1:7:

> For God did not give us a spirit of fear, but a
> spirit of power, of love, and of self-discipline.
> (KJV)

Hallelujah! God did not give us a spirit of fear-timidity; but, a spirit of power, love and self-discipline. If you are in Christ, you have God's ability to live a disciplined life. Think about that. You have God's ability in you. We are called to live like Jesus here in this earth realm, exactly like Him. Jesus did good, loved and cared for those He met and so can we.

How to Transform Thinking

We saw in the scriptures that God has given us self-discipline and self-control. So why aren't we living in it? Here's something we need to understand, to be disciplined or to be undisciplined starts in the mind: through the thought process. If you are undisciplined in your thinking, you will be undisciplined in how you live your life.

The Bible says in Colossians 2:15 "When He had disarmed the rulers and authorities [those supernatural forces of evil operating against us], He made a public example of them [exhibiting them as captives in His triumphal procession], having triumphed over them through [a]the cross." Since Christ triumphed over the enemy, the only way the enemy can attack us is in the mind. The enemy—satan—attacks us through our soul (mind, will, emotions, intellect, imaginations and memory). We can close or open the door to him by controlling our thoughts or letting them run rampant and unchecked. To close the door, Paul says the believer is to be renewed in the spirit of the mind—"be ye transformed by the renewing of your mind" (Rom. 12:2 KJV). What is Paul talking about? He's talking about how you think. Again, your life will follow the direction of your thinking. If you will renew your mind, renovate it, you can change your life for good! Bad habits, drug addictions, sexual addictions, depression, bad attitudes, fear, anxiety, all can be destroyed! Rather than continuing to do the same thing over and over and expecting different results, stop the problem where it starts: in the mind.

Disciplined thinking results in a disciplined life. So, your thinking determines the measure of the discipline that will be established in your life.

Some examples of areas we must use discipline include getting up early in the morning, reading, praying, dealing wisely with our finances, eating healthy, and having a good attitude. Where does each start? In the mind—how and what you think about it. Have you ever thought about what you think about? I believe we would be shocked what we allow ourselves to think sometimes.

Many of the negative issues we may have stem from what we think about ourselves. Some people have such low self-esteem about themselves that it's almost a shame. On the other hand, others have an overrated opinion about themselves until it's a shame. We can only find the balance by meditating God's Word, being filled and led by the Spirit of God.

I believe that bad relationships are the results of bad thinking just as good relationships are the results of good thinking. This is true of the marriage relationships. Negative thoughts, especially uncontrolled thoughts, about your spouse will lead to a bad relationship. The enemy puts pressure on those kinds of relationships, simply because he wants believers to abort them or he wants to cause chaos inside them. There are relationships we must value enough to fight for and keep them from being chaotic and/or aborted. Why? Because our destiny is tied to human relationships. We can't do this life by ourselves. No Lone Rangers! Deny yourself so that God may be glorified in your relationships. It would take me a while to tell you how my wife and I had to discipline ourselves, how we had to go to the Word to keep chaos out and not to run from the relationship! We both wanted to please God so we went to God's will, His order and government which we found in His Word. And, thank God for the Holy Spirit, our Helper and Strengthener.

Consider what Paul says in 2 Corinthians 10:4–6:

> (For the weapons of our warfare are not carnal, but mighty through God to the pulling down of strong holds;) Casting down imaginations, and every high thing that exalteth itself against the knowledge of God, and bringing into captivity every thought to the obedience of Christ; And having in a readiness to revenge all disobedience, when your obedience is fulfilled. (KJV)

Notice in verse 4, Paul talks about the weapons of our warfare. In Ephesians chapter 6, Paul writes about this same idea, saying believers don't fight against flesh and blood, but against principalities and powers. Paul is talking about spirits that rule in the spirit realm. Most of the issues that people deal with do not come out of the natural realm, but out of the spiritual realm. Humans view everything from a natural point, rather than a supernatural view; thus, they become the casualty in spiritual warfare against the enemy. Our lack of understanding of what is happening in the spirit world, the unseen and a lack of self-discipline often block the victory, the win, that God has given us. The enemy counts on us being undisciplined in going to the Word and in our thoughts. A man who is disciplined to the degree that he's exercising and looking good, slim and trim, is classified as disciplined. Rightly so, but where did it start? In the gym? No, it began in his mind, with a change in his thinking.

Let's go back to our text scripture, Romans 12:2 (AMP):

> Do not be conformed to this world (this age), [fashioned after and adapted to its external, superficial customs], but be transformed (changed) by the [entire] renewal of your mind [by its new ideals and its new attitude], so that you may prove [for yourselves] what is the good and acceptable and perfect will of God, even the thing which is good and acceptable and perfect [in His sight for you].

To exchange our way for God's way, we need to understand His role as God. He is our Father—the initiator of our relationship with Him. He is the One Who gave His life for us. He is the One who delivered us from the power of darkness and translated us into the Kingdom of His dear Son. He knows what's best for us. We must come to the point of valuing Him and His Word. So, let's view some scriptures:

Isaiah 55:8 (KJV)

For my thoughts are not your thoughts, neither are your ways my ways, saith the Lord.

John 6:63 (KJV)

It is the spirit that quickeneth; the flesh profiteth nothing: the words that I speak unto you, they are spirit, and they are life.

2 Timothy 3:16 (AMPC)

Every Scripture is God-breathed (given by His inspiration) and profitable for instruction, for reproof and conviction of sin, for correction of error and discipline in obedience, [and] for training in righteousness (in holy living, in conformity to God's will in thought, purpose, and action),

2 Timothy 3:16 (MSG)

Every part of Scripture is God-breathed and useful one way or another—showing us truth, exposing our rebellion, correcting our mistakes, training us to live God's way. Through the Word we are put together and shaped up for the tasks God has for us.

Let's draw a principle from Proverbs of the impact of Scripture, if we will take it and put in our hearts and minds.

Proverbs 3:1–2 (AMPC)
My son, forget not my law or teaching, but let your heart keep my commandments;
For length of days and years of a life [worth living] and tranquility [inward and outward and continuing through old age till death], these shall they add to you.

There is a three-fold application in renewing the mind completely—to change your thinking: meditate the Word, speak the Word and act on the Word.

Meditation is the master key to transforming the mind. Meditation implies to mutter, to speak it to ourselves, over and over again. This is not a religious or evil act; but a spiritual one based in the Word of God.

Let's take Joshua for an example. After Moses, the servant of God died, God gave Joshua an assignment. To accomplish it, Joshua would have to meditate on the Word God had spoken to him. Joshua 1:8 (KJV) states

"This book of the law shall not depart out of thy mouth; but thou shalt meditate therein day and night, that thou mayest observe to do according to all that is written therein: for

then thou shalt make thy way prosperous,
and then thou shalt have good success."

Because God knew there would be challenges for
Joshua to take the land, in Joshua1:6, God told him
to "be strong and of good courage". Then, in verse 7,
he told Joshua again, "be strong and very courageous".
Then in verse 9, it states, "Have not I commanded thee?
Be strong and of a good courage; be not afraid, neither
be thou dismayed: for the Lord thy God is with thee
whithersoever thou goest."

I believe the Lord was having Joshua meditate those
words and the more He said it to Joshua, the more
Joshua would think about, would meditate it. He would
speak it to himself over and over and over. As Joshua
was meditating the Word of God, the Holy Spirit was
building that image in Joshua's heart and mind. The
more he meditated it, the more he turned it over in his
heart and mind, the more he spoke it to himself, the
more he could get a glimpse of him doing that Word.
The more he meditated it, the bigger and clearer the
picture of himself taking the land got inside him. As the
Holy Spirit worked in Joshua, in his spirit, that Word
created a picture, an image, in Joshua's mind. This is
called a process. Then in verse 10, we see Joshua doing
the Word. He was bold and strong and he commanded
the officers as God has said.

That was old testament! If we would meditate the Word, being under the new covenant, we will have God results too. It is a principle and it will work every time! When we mediate the Word of God, put it in us in abundance, the same Holy Spirit, will work in us to transform our minds. He will use the Word to create the image of that Word in us. We will see ourselves doing and having what the Word says. Then we will begin to speak it and do it! For the Bible declares for out of the abundance of the heart, the mouth will speak.

Again, I must reiterate the law of consistency. It is consistency that will produce life change. The reality is that we all meditate on something. Do you know that worrying is a form of meditation? You have people who will meditate, which means to mutter, to turn it over and over and over again, to speak it to themselves, that they won't have enough money to pay a bill at the end of the month. They talk about it, they think about it, they can't even sleep. They get anxiety attacks about it. Why? They are worrying which is a form of meditation, in a negative sense. Let's turn that around. Get God's proven Word and meditate it. He is Truth. He is not a God that He would lie. His Word will stand the test of time.

Weapons of Warfare

Notice in verse 4 Paul talks about the *weapons* of warfare and what these weapons are used for: pulling down strongholds. Strongholds are thoughts, imaginations, or ideas that we have grown up with or picked up from our environment which govern the way we think and therefore, govern our lives. They are embedded ways of thinking. Our environment, society, our associations are some of the influences which impacted our thought process along the way. Think back to your childhood, and recall any acts, words or experiences that happened to you which may have influenced your imaginations, ideas and attitudes in both a negative and a positive way. When you grow up with these imaginations, thoughts, or ideas, they are a part of you. They govern the way you think; therefore, they govern your life, whether positively or negatively.

Because those ways of thinking have become a part of us, it may be years before we discover the negative ones. We just think that's the way it is. You believe your way of thinking is "normal." Yet, it could be so far from the truth! So, God, in His infinite wisdom had Hebrews 4:12 (AMP) written for us:

> For the Word that God speaks is alive and full of power [making it active, operative, energizing, and effective]; it is sharper than any two-edged sword, penetrating to the dividing

line of the [a]breath of life (soul) and [the immortal] spirit, and of joints and marrow [of the deepest parts of our nature], exposing and sifting and analyzing and judging the very thoughts and purposes of the heart.

Now notice the words in this scripture: "The Word that God speaks is alive and full of power." Alive means it moves, it has life! It also has the power in it to divide (to separate) what is our way and what is God's way. That's why the enemy, satan, fights so hard for us to become Word people. Notice, I didn't say "church people" but "Word people." But you must be determined. Approach the Bible with an open, honest heart and when reading it, say, "That's me." Then, thank the Lord for revealing anything that needs to be changed.

Remember these thoughts, imaginations, and ideas exalt themselves *against* the will of God for your lie. Since the will of God is His Word, we will use the Word to destroy the opposing thoughts. We will also use the Name and Blood of Jesus as weapons of warfare. Since you were created in God's image, when you speak the Word in faith, you can expect the same results the Father got. The words you speak will be alive and full of power.

If we yield to thoughts that oppose God's will it can make us an *outlaw* in the realm of the spirit. But, when we give the Word and the Holy Spirit their rightful place, we close the door and we win.

Jesus told Simon Peter this once: "Simon, Simon, Satan has asked to sift each of you like wheat. But I have prayed for you, Simon, that your faith will not fail" (Luke 22:31 NLT). Satan is still arguing that he has the right to do what he wants to do in believers because they have something in them that belongs to him. But the believer's job is to pray that their faith will not fail. The devil shouldn't be able to touch the believer's life or even to get into their life or in their business at will. But, uncontrolled thoughts and imaginations give him that access—now he has a right.

So warfare is in the mind—in the area of your thinking. In 2 Corinthians 10:5–6 Paul writes that there are thoughts, imaginations, and ideas that have to be dealt with. Those that are truly saved have the Spirit of Christ, who gives witness that certain thoughts aren't right. So we can know by the Word and the witness if thoughts are against or in agreement with the will of God. The only way to know if thoughts and thought patterns are wrong or right is by saturating ourselves in the Word of God and allow the Word to work in us. The Word is the only measuring stick that believers have for what's right and what's wrong. We are not called to live by opinions, but by what is Truth—not our truth, but God's Truth. St. John 17:17 "Sanctify them through thy truth: thy word is truth."

Sometimes people are so overwhelmed emotionally, however, that they pay no attention to that witness. The

Spirit's voice is brushed off, and other thoughts, those embedded thoughts and thought patterns, remain the basis for what is true.

One of the things that has blessed me is the fact that I have a wife that's in the Word as much as I am and she will voice when she sees me reacting in wrong, ungodly ways. "Now you know better than that," she'll say. And I'll respond, "You're right I do". She helps to pull me to my senses—my spiritual senses.

The worst thing close friends or family can do is endorse your wrong thinking.

The Bible says, "A person may think their own ways are right, but the LORD weighs the heart" (Prov. 21:2). Everybody thinks they're right, and no one ever thinks that they are wrong. The Word of God is the measuring stick.

Notes

Chapter 5

——◆——

Environment, Imagination and Influence

God the Father is trying to break into His people's world—each and every person who is a follower of Christ. He wants to fulfill every promise He has made to us. The blessing, the empowerment to prosper and succeed, is on the believer; but, God wants to show us how to live in the blessing.

Let's go to 2 Corinthians 10:4–6:

> (For the weapons of our warfare are not carnal, but mighty through God to the pulling down of strong holds;) Casting down imaginations, and every high thing that exalteth itself against the knowledge of God, and bringing into captivity every thought to the obedience of Christ; And having in a readiness to revenge all disobedience, when your obedience is fulfilled. (KJV)

Let's look at 2 Corinthians 10:5 (AMP)

> *We are* destroying sophisticated arguments
> and every exalted *and* proud thing that sets
> itself up against the [true] knowledge of God,
> and *we are* taking every thought *and* purpose
> captive to the obedience of Christ, (AMP)

Paul was teaching the Corinthian church to recognize and destroy imaginations and proud arguments that try to exalt themselves against the true knowledge of God. Because he understood the danger of allowing those truths to remain unchecked, he told them to do something about it.

These thoughts, imaginations and ideas main objective is to lead you away, a little at a time, from God's *perfect* will for your life. When you entertain them, he gets a toe in. The more you sit and entertain it, the bigger his will becomes in your life. And, then one day, you sit and say, "What happened?" It started way back when the first thought was not checked. In Psalms 1:1–3, we are warned about this as well:

> Blessed is the man that walketh not in the
> counsel of the ungodly, nor standeth in the
> way of sinners, nor sitteth in the seat of the
> scornful.
> But his delight is in the law of the LORD; and
> in his law doth he meditate day and night.

And he shall be like a tree planted by the rivers of water, that bringeth forth his fruit in his season; his leaf also shall not wither; and whatsoever he doeth shall prosper.

We must be alert at all times and ready at all times to control our thoughts. How can we be ready? By being in good spiritual shape, good spiritual condition. We must do our spiritual "exercise" daily—study and meditate the Word, praying in the Spirit, praise and worship, confessing the Word and acting on the Word.

Here's what the Bible says: give the devil no place! Resist him and the Bible says he will flee from you. (James 4:7). He can't just overpower or overtake you. He has to do it through your thoughts. So every thought that comes to your mind is not your thought. He will try to sow seeds of discord, strife, bitterness, unforgiveness, and fear and much more. But, because you are in good spiritually shape, ready for battle, you recognize it is a weapon of the enemy and he wants you to accept it. But, you realize you can refuse delivery! Tell him "take it back, in Jesus Name." Then declare what God's Word says about the situation. I remember a man of God say don't go after the enemy with your mouth shut. You must speak the Word. To speak the Word, you must know the Word. And, not just know the Word in the sense of just quoting it; but it must be in your heart. Remember the scripture says, out of the abundance of the heart the mouth will speak.

Strongholds

Strongholds never fall or lay down of their own accord. They have to be pulled down. Even after a person is saved, the possibility of strongholds could be there in their life. When Paul was writing this letter, he was writing to the church at Corinth, which had many problems. People were giving their lives to Jesus but their lives weren't changing. They were still doing all the things they were doing before they got saved. They had the same attitudes, the same disposition, and the same habits. No doubt Christ was their Savior, but for some reason, their lives were not being transformed. Their lives were not reflecting Jesus. If Paul could visit the church of the Lord Jesus Christ today, would he see the same thing he saw in Corinth?

There's a strong possibility that strongholds have remained unchecked in today's church which have prevented many from standing in their God-given potential. Those strongholds are not going to just walk out. They have to be pulled down. "Pulling" in that 2 Corinthians 10:4–6 implies "demolition." And demolition means "tearing something down, to destroy." The believer is to destroy the strongholds that keep them in bondage!

Notice that strongholds are of a spiritual nature. Notice how Paul starts off verse 4: "For the weapons of our warfare are not carnal . . ."

The Spiritual Nature of Strongholds

There is nothing physical or natural a Christian can do to *destroy* a stronghold. Somewhere down the line, they must be spiritually minded to engage and demolish a stronghold. Because a stronghold is of a spiritual nature, there is the possibility of demonic activity. I don't believe that a Christian can be possessed by the devil because to be possessed means to be fully in-filled. It is not possible to have the life and nature of God in a person, and the devil at the same time. But there is a possibility of demonic *influence*. Remember satan exalted himself above God. Selfishness is at the root of his influences. He wants you to please yourself. It's all about you. That directly opposes God's way. God says to deny yourself. He says if you seek Him and His way of doing He will add all good things to us (Matthew 6:33). But the enemy would want us to think God is holding good things from us. That's a lie.

There were so many things that looked cool to me that really made me a fool when it came down to my life in Christ. I remember when I first came into the church, I didn't know anything about lifting my hands and my attitude was, "I'm not lifting my hands." What did I look like? In the presence of God, I would keep my hands down and I would sit there and look at other people lift their hands. To me, I looked cool, but in the spirit, what did I look like? I didn't know,

I Timothy 2:8 which says: " I will therefore that men pray everywhere, lifting up holy hands, without wrath and doubting."

If an attitude or idea doesn't line up with the Scripture, God does not accept it. So, we must be teachable and come to the point of saying, "I am crucified with Christ: nevertheless I live; yet not I, but Christ liveth in me: and the life which I now live in the flesh I live by the faith of the Son of God, who loved me, and gave himself for me." (Galatians 2:20)

If God says to do it, then that's what He delights in. He doesn't delight in all of us doing our own thing or own way. Can you imagine what chaos that would be?

Now here's a question we must ask ourselves: where is that thought coming from? I believe it is so important that we develop spiritually so we can recognize the source of thoughts immediately. Become such a student of the Word of God that you can judge the source and nature of every thought.

The Carnal Mind is Proof of the Need for Change

Let's go to Romans 8:6–8

For to be carnally minded is death; but to be spiritually minded is life and peace. Because the carnal mind is enmity against God: for it is not subject to the law of God, neither deed can be. So, then they that are in the flesh cannot please God.

The Bible talks about 3 minds: the natural mind, the carnal mind and the spiritual (renewed) mind. The person that is not born again has a natural mind. The Christian, who has not renewed his mind, has a carnal mind. Lastly, the Christian, who has exercised himself in those spiritual things (meditating the Word, confessing the Word and acting on the Word) has the spiritual, renewed mind.

The carnal minded person constantly says, "See this is the way I do it." It is hostile to the things of God. So every Christian should be committed to transforming their thinking.

Let's reads Romans 8:6–8 again.

> For to be carnally minded is death; but to be spiritually minded is life and peace. Because the carnal mind is enmity against God: for it is not subject to the law of God, neither deed can be. So, then they that are in the flesh cannot please God. (KJV)

Do you want to be a Christian who enjoys life and peace? Then renew your mind to the Word of God. Do you want to be a Christian whose thinking is enmity (opposing) to God? Then renew your mind to the Word of God. Paul says he became a slave unto Christ—to doing things His way. Jesus says, "You shall know the truth." Now if you know the truth and do the truth, you are free.

I remember when I would catch a cold as a child. My little grandmother would purchase Castrol Oil and something called three 6's. It was the nastiest stuff I ever tasted in the world, but in about 3–4 hours I felt better. Truth that challenges your way of thinking can be tough, but it will give you a better life!

Paul speaks about the believer's thoughts in 2 Corinthians 10:5–6:

> Casting down imaginations, and every high thing that exalteth itself against the knowledge of God, and bringing into captivity every thought to the obedience of Christ; And having in a readiness to revenge all disobedience, when your obedience is fulfilled. (KJV)

Believers are saved through grace by faith, but casting down imaginations and bringing them into captivity is a process. This can only happen by meditating on and studying the Word. Now that sounds simple but that's more than a notion. It's a fight to get into the Word because it is a fight against deep-seeded thought habits.

Imaginations and ideas can excite certain emotions. Emotions are born through thoughts. Feelings are born through thoughts. Therefore , what you allow yourself to think is important.

In the earlier chapter, I mentioned that it was important to understand that we are spirit beings. We possess a soul and live in a body. We are to live from our spirit. If we forget that we are spirit beings, we will be passive about things we should not be. When we compare the fruit of the carnal mind and the fruit of the spiritual mind, we should make a choice to do those things that lead to a spiritual mind. We are commanded to choose life! And, we must have corresponding actions that align with that choice.

Meditation and study start with having a good pastor who is filled with and yielded to the Holy Spirit. Believers who are not connected to a good church (even if they go to church) will find it impossible to win this battle. The Bible says those who are planted in the house of God shall flourish.

The Cost of Following Christ

Now committing oneself to anything always costs something. I know people don't like to commit themselves because of the cost. But, if you will take the time to compare the benefits and the negatives (count up the costs), you will find commitment to God's ways is worth it! Until you are willing to see the benefits of connection from God's viewpoint, you will not connect. When you stay in a carnal mindset, you will deem commitment to God *and* His ways, order and government as unimportant, not necessary, not priority. It's like when New Year's Day comes. People make resolutions that they will do this and they will do that, but they only do it for two to three weeks. They have good intentions; but no commitment.

Paul had a Pastors Conference where he gave pastors advice and insight on their responsibility and accountability as under-shepherds to God's people. Let's go to Acts 20:28 to see what happened:

> Take care *and* be on guard for yourselves and for the whole flock over which the Holy Spirit has appointed you as overseers, to shepherd (tend, feed, guide) the church of God which He bought with His own blood. (AMPC)

Paul is revealing a principle of God—that men and women of God should take care of their spiritual life first and then the flock (church).

No one belongs to the pastor; they belong to Jesus. People believe they can take care of themselves in the natural. They can to some degree. However, based on this scripture, God appointed pastors to help care for the spiritual needs of His people.

We saw in Paul's pastors' meeting that the Holy Ghost is the one who appoints the shepherds. God calls them and the Holy Ghost appoints them. Now let's go to another pastor's meeting, in 1 Peter 5:1–4:

Therefore, I strongly urge the elders among you [pastors, spiritual leaders of the church], as a fellow elder and as an eyewitness [called to testify] of the sufferings of Christ, as well as one who shares in the glory that is to be revealed: shepherd *and* guide *and* protect the flock of God among you, exercising oversight not under compulsion, but voluntarily, according to *the will of* God; and not [motivated] for shameful gain, but with wholehearted enthusiasm; not lording it over those assigned to your care [do not be arrogant or overbearing], but be examples [of Christian living] to the flock [set a pattern of integrity for your congregation]. And when the Chief Shepherd (Christ) appears, you will receive the [conqueror's] unfading crown of glory. (AMPC)

These scriptures reveal God's heart toward His people-His church. It also reveals the responsibility of the Pastor. Paul tells the elders they need to watch over God's people, have a good attitude toward them and not take advantage of them. This is serious business. So, the man of God must be yielded to the Holy Spirit to do this.

Let's go to Ephesians 4:8:

Therefore it is said, When He ascended on high, He led captivity captive [He led a train

of vanquished foes] and He bestowed gifts
on men. (AMPC)

But there are certain things a believer cannot get
done until there is a connection. Your leader has to
pour things in you and you have to receive what he's
pouring before that operation can take place in your
life in a real way.

Let's go to Ephesians 4:11–12 AMPC

> And His gifts were [varied; He Himself
> appointed and gave men to us] some to be
> apostles (special messengers), some prophets
> (inspired preachers and expounders), some
> evangelists (preachers of the Gospel, travel-
> ing missionaries), some pastors (shepherds
> of His flock) and teachers.
> His intention was the perfecting and the full
> equipping of the saints (His consecrated
> people), [that they should do] the work of
> ministering toward building up Christ's body
> (the church),

The word "perfecting" implies "maturing." To help
with the maturing process, God, put His system, His
order, in place. He chose to use men and women of
God. He chose to anoint them as His mouthpiece.
Now the devil doesn't want believers to connect with
other believers for many reasons—which is why it is

so important to make a connection! It is so important for believers to become spiritually minded. Pray and ask God where He wants you planted. You can use the scripture in I Corinthian 12:18 as a basis for your prayer:

> But now hath God set the members every one
> of them in the body, as it hath pleased him.

Once you have the witness, get settled, remained there and be fruitful. Deny yourself. Deny your thoughts that exalt itself against the knowledge of God. I remember a book I read years ago called Fit, Function and Flourish. Psalm 92:13 says, "Those that be planted in the house of the LORD shall flourish in the courts of our God." As an act of your will and with the help of the Holy Spirit, submit to those in authority at that church because that's where you will flourish. Your gifts will be revealed and developed and you will be a blessing to the Kingdom. In addition, you will learn how to appropriate the blessings of God in your life! But again, what will deter a person from getting planted, making the proper connection? It's a direct result of how a person thinks. But, once the believer gets his or her thinking in line with God's Word, they will put their roots down and be about the Father's business.

From an age(number) standpoint, a person may be considered mature; but that is not true spiritually. Believers, regardless of age, must be teachable to grow up in the Lord Jesus. When people come into churches they have their own ideas and thoughts of how they think things should be. It doesn't work like that. The Holy Spirit made the pastor, the overseer. So the Holy Spirit first feeds the pastor. Then the pastor can teach others. We have all had ideas about church and the preacher's role, since we were young. And, some were down right wrong. But it was a plan of the enemy to keep us from reaching our full potential in Christ. He planted those seeds early on in life. I always use the example of a doctor. You can hear about doctors getting sued for giving the wrong medicine. Yet, we still go to doctors. We don't throw them all away. Yet, the devil will tell people that all preachers are wrong. If that is the case, then God would be wrong. If you sincerely want to know God and His way, because God is love, He will see to it that you meet someone, some kind of way, to get you on the right path. It will cost us being teachable enough to yield to God's way. It will cost you discipline. It will cause denying yourself to reach for the greater.

In God's infinite wisdom, he knew the two-fold ministry was important to our growth and development: the ministry gifts in Ephesians 4 and the Holy Spirit.

The Process of Casting Down Imaginations, Thoughts and Ideas

Let's go back to II Corinthians 10:4–6:

> (For the weapons of our warfare are not carnal, but mighty through God to the pulling down of strong holds;) Casting down imaginations, and every high thing that exalteth itself against the knowledge of God, and bringing into captivity every thought to the obedience of Christ; And having in a readiness to revenge all disobedience, when your obedience is fulfilled. (KJV)

As we mentioned before, even though a person has become a new creation, it's a challenge to think like one. We have to deal with those embedded ways of thinking. To demolish, destroy the imaginations, thoughts that exalt itself against the will of God, we must enter into the mind renewal process by meditation— studying, confessing and acting on the Word.

Let's look closer at what we should meditate. There are a lot of things we can meditate on and study. The enemy will work to get us off track and have us study things that aren't important or to study things out of order/priority. This is not productive. Believers will never fulfill their purpose in Christ by doing whatever they want to do. God has a set order and a set pattern for Christians to follow. It is outlined in His Word, and it is important to be disciplined enough to follow.

When God places a person in a local church, it's all about purpose and destiny.

Remember 1 Corinthians 12:18, God says He places us in the body as it pleases Him. He places each one of us in the right place, the right church, the right family to help His plan to come to pass.

There are thousands upon thousands of Christians looking for a place (a church) that's suitable for them. But often they are looking at the outer things (like how big the choir is, how big building is, how long the service) and totally ignore the spiritual. From those peripheral things, they determine if that's the church they should be attending. But a person's heart, influenced by the Holy Spirit, is what should tell them where they should be. If you are a floater, stop now and get God's mindset. Become spiritually minded in this area. You are missing out on God's best and being the blessing God wants you to be. Refuse to be an outlaw in this area. If I were you, I wouldn't spend another moment without seeking God about this because time is precious.

Let's get back to determine what we should meditate on. Jeremiah 3:15 (KJV) states,

> And I will give you pastors according to mine heart, which shall feed you with knowledge and understanding.

Notice the verse makes some profound statements. Number one, the pastors are after God's heart. This should do away with every thought that says all Pastors are bad or want your money, etc. That can't be true and God's word be true. Number two, the pastors are supposed to feed you. So if they are to feed you, then that means, you must come to eat. Number three, pastors should feed you with knowledge and understanding. This means spiritual knowledge and understanding.

When we are fed the Word of God, we are supposed to chew it, like you chew gum. Look at Mark 4:24 (AMP):

> And he said unto them, Be careful what you are hearing. The measure (of thought and study) you give to the truth you hear) will be the measure (of virtue, and knowledge) that comes back to you—and more besides will be given to you who hear.

Jesus said we should meditate and study the truths we hear. Hear from whom? The pastors God gave who are after His heart and who are commanded to feed us His Word.

I remember when I asked God, "Father, why do you use men to teach us the Gospel?" He said, "Do you realize everyone starts off as babe?" He said to me, "I use men because they can get my message, my plan to the babes to the point that they will grow and develop spiritually. See babes need things they can touch and feel and see."

He said, "If I (God) minister directly to them, they would be confused. I need you to build the foundation. I need you to feed them knowledge and understanding about Me. They can see you and touch you. As they grow and develop, they learn how to relate to Me."

1 Peter 2:2 proves that we are babies in Christ and it is the milk of the Word that produces growth. It states, "As newborn babes, desire the sincere milk of the word, that ye may grow thereby:"

It is important to understand that teachings come from the Holy Spirit, but God uses men to convey these messages. The pastor, by the Holy Spirit, will pull the milk out of the Word for you. Babes in Christ can become overwhelmed by thoughts, imaginations and ideas that the enemy sends. If there is no one to help them, they will often shut down.

Now some people think they want meat all the time. But the Bible says, the meat is for the spiritually mature (Hebrews 5:14).

The mind can be renewed in one area and unrenewed in another area. This is why preaching and teaching are necessary—it is like food to eat and water to drink. Without teachings of God's Word, life will be the teacher—and that can dangerous. Preaching and teaching are designed to inspire us to grow and develop spiritually. As a preacher and pastor, I can see this. There are many Christians who have walked with Jesus for years and yet are undeveloped spiritually. But how a person chooses to live their life speaks volumes. Victories and defeats say something about a person's life. Each seed produces after its own kind. Take a personal inventory of life; it will show you how you think. Remember what Paul said: "When I was a child, I spoke and thought and reasoned as a child. But when I grew up, I put away childish things" (1 Cor. 13:11 NLT).

There are certain things that can't be put away without growing up. And God is patient with us, yet His heart is longing for us to grow because He needs us to show His love to others. He needs us to stand in the authority He has given and take authority over the works of the enemy. Developing spiritually is a personal decision. Because your spiritual food—teaching and preaching—is vital for your spiritual growth, you should not practice missing church. If you don't eat your spiritual food and chew it properly, you will not grow properly.

Offices Within the Church

Now let's look at the work of the pastor. People see pastors totally opposite of the Word of God. The devil has painted such a bad picture of pastors that it's pathetic. I do understand that men are imperfect and some have not stood in the office as honorably as they should. But I want to give God's perspective to the pastor's office that He has given. The pastoral ministry is primarily responsible for the *spiritual* growth and development of the church. When I say that, I'm not talking about numbers. I'm talking about people in the church growing up and maturing in Christ. And that's what God awaits—His people's maturity.

Let's view Ephesians 4:11–12 (KJV)

> And he gave some, apostles; and some, prophets; and some, evangelists; and some, pastors and teachers;
> For the perfecting of the saints, for the work of the ministry, for the edifying of the body of Christ:

When we take the time to meditate these scriptures, we can see just how purposeful God is. These ministry gifts were given for the perfecting(maturing) of the saints, for the work of ministry and for the edifying of the body of Christ. These ministry gifts function differently but the purpose is the same. Apostles, pastors, and teachers carry the weight of growth and development for the maturing of the saints. The evangelist is the person that stirs people hearts so they can receive Jesus Christ as Savior. The prophet is the one who inspires the church. Apostles are mainly people who set order—not *their* order, but God's order. They plant churches and establish the people in a solid foundation of Christian truths.

The pastors are always with the flock—day and night. They are responsible for teaching and preaching the Word so God's children can come to a place of maturity.

Nobody is born again in a spiritually mature state. Yes, a person can be mature naturally (according to their age) but may not be spiritually mature because there is a process called growth. If a person can't stay steady for long, this is a strong indication they are still a babe.

Two character traits of babes in Christ are envy and strife. Babes do nothing but fight. Some fight against God. Have you ever tried to feed a baby something healthy that maybe he doesn't like? He just fights and fights. This also happens spiritually. That's why pastors and all ministry gifts should entrust the Holy Spirit to give them the message (spiritual food) for God's people.

Now the thing about a babe is: a babe that's been a babe a long time can't be convinced he's a babe. He will fight you on that issue. But the fruit is there. Therefore, God, tempers the pastors with a shepherd's heart, to exercise patience and love, that will be needed as the babies are growing.

While all the ministry gifts play a part in helping the church grow spiritually, the Pastor has the greatest responsibility in this area . Now I've been pastoring thirty years, but when I started, I shouldn't have. I was called to it but I didn't have the maturity for it. I should have been under a mentor. I needed to learn from others who understood the deeper things of Christ before I took on pastoring by myself.

Positioning yourself under another spiritually mature person who knows and understands the process will help you tremendously. Spiritual maturity can happen without a mentor, but the process will be slower—as will the effectiveness and the success. To submit to another ministry gift, takes the proper attitude of the heart.

Now, let's look at Acts 20:28:

> Take care *and* be on guard for yourselves and the whole flock over which the Holy Spirit has appointed you bishops and guardians, to shepherd (tend and feed and guide) the church of the Lord *or of God* which He obtained for Himself [buying it and saving it for Himself] with His own blood. (AMP)

Paul exhorts and reminds the pastors to take care of their own spiritual affairs and to take oversight over the flock which the Holy Spirit appointed them. Now from this scripture, you can see there should not be any self-appointed pastors if we are going to follow God's orders. Then he says: to tend, feed and guide the ones whom He purchased with His blood. This sounds serious to me.

Therefore, I refuse to pastor according to my opinions or the opinions of others. Following opinions that are opposite of God's will guarantee a sure shipwreck. Yielding to the Holy Spirit guarantees success.

When Moses passed on, God said He was going to put the same spirit that was on Moses on the people.

Thus, congregants can't work with the pastor and fight him at the same time. Brother Hagin said something that blessed my life, and to this day I live within this truth. He said, "When a man intrudes into the wrong office, he can die premature." I believe those that are "after God's heart" carry a humility with them because they realize they have been honored by God to stand in that position. They also understand the responsibility and accountability that go along with the office.

A pastor is a bishop and a guardian. "Bishop" simply means "overseer." The overseer takes responsibility for the well-being of those under his care and authority. Whether one knows it or not, everyone needs some-body to be responsible for their spiritual growth and development. The Holy Spirit says He appoints pastors to be responsible for the flock well-being spiritually (not naturally).

A guardian is someone legally in charge of the affairs of a minor or a person of an unsound mind. A minor is a young person— someone who is not fully mature and developed yet and who doesn't have the capacity to make sound decisions on his or her own. Babies have an unsound spiritual mind; meaning, their minds or thinking is not solidly based on the foundation of God's Word. They tend to make choices that are pleasing at the *moment*. They just know, I want it! So, the pastor has been commissioned by God to tend, feed and guide the baby in Christ in the Word.

Some may say they don't need a pastor—but in reality, they do. Remember, babies, adolescent, teenagers often feel they don't need their parents. But it isn't true. Without a pastor, a believer can't grow and develop spiritually properly. Now, I didn't say they can't grow and develop spiritually. I said they won't grow and develop properly. Why? They are outside of God's order. It doesn't matter how we think we are growing. It doesn't matter if everybody, including the President, applaud you. If God has not applauded, you are missing the mark. And, those efforts are "strange fire" to God.

I say to the men and women of God, know who called and appointed you. Go to the Word. If someone asks, "Who qualified you?" My answer would be, "The Holy Spirit!" I know this is pretty straight forward. But, it is time for us to get the mind of Christ, grow up and do what God said to do.

Now, let's read to Hebrews 5:13:

> For every one that useth milk is unskilful in the
> Word of righteousness: for he is a babe. (KJV)

Babes are unskillful in the Word. Would anyone bring a baby home and tell them, there's the bed, and there's the refrigerator, get what you want? No. Spiritual babes are similar; they can't feed themselves yet.

> Casting down imaginations, and every high
> thing that exalteth itself against the knowl-

edge of God, and bringing into captivity every thought to the obedience of Christ; And having in a readiness to revenge all disobedience, when your obedience is fulfilled.

~ 2 Corinthians 10:5–6 KJV

A babe can't cast down those thoughts, imaginations and ideas that have been with him for so long. He has the ability to cast down the thoughts. But, he doesn't have the understanding and knowledge of how to operate in that ability yet. I have two sons, who are eight years apart. When the younger one was growing up, he saw the older one do things, and he tried to do it, but he couldn't do it. He had the ability to do things, but he didn't have the maturity to do it. Babes in Christ don't have the maturity to operate in certain spiritual principles. Therefore, God gives them a pastor—an undershepherd—to teach and train them. That is why I call the church "God's schoolhouse of learning."

How Does the Pastor Take Care of the Spiritual Affairs of Babes?

The pastor cares for the spiritual affairs of babes by prevailing in prayer. Pastors should be people of prayer and they hold people up before God. Paul says to pray for them until Christ is formed in them (Galatians 4:19). I pray that God will open up their eyes of understanding

(Ephesians 1:18). See I can't just preach and cause people to go where they need to go. Preaching is only a part of the process. Sometimes I need to spend some serious time, holding someone up before God, praying for them, calling their name, praying that their eyes of understanding are being enlightened, and praying that they be filled with the full knowledge of God's will and all wisdom and understanding (Colossians 1:9). See I can pray for others when I can't talk to them. I pray for them when I see them acting outside of God's perfect plan for them.

As I pray, the Holy Spirit reveals the tactic the devil is trying to use to get them off track. As I stand in the gap and make up the hedge for them, I believe the Holy Spirit is ministering to them, helping them to win. I preach to people and pray for them. That's how I take care of their spiritual affairs. I'm appointed and anointed to pray. I'm appointed and anointed to teach. And often people don't make it easy. But it's ok, because my supply is from the Holy Spirit. Remember, God calls and appoints Pastors. God anoints them. He provides to them what is needed to care for His people. Pastors should know it is not in their own strength that they do what they do. But, God is their Source. Then they will care for God's precious people the way He wants.

Feeding them properly, the right diet, is important to God. He knows that His Word is the Sword of the Spirit and will defeat every tactic of the enemy. He knows if you can change the way you think, you can change your life! Here's a famous quote that is worth stating:

> "Watch your thoughts; they become words.
> Watch your words; they become actions.
> Watch your actions; they become habits.
> Watch your habits; they become character.
> Watch your character; it becomes your destiny."

Notes

Conclusion

As I wrote this book, I wrote it with passion because I know personally, the necessity and challenge that is in changing the way you think. I also know the sweet victory it brought to my life and family.

To be born again, to become children of God, we must accept Jesus Christ as our Savior (Romans 10:9–10). When we are born again, we become a new creation in Christ Jesus. We become a part of God's family. Romans 5:18 says, we have been adopted and we can now call God, Abba Father.

Now that we are a part of God's family, we must not stop there. Yes, we are saved. Yes, we are on our way to heaven. But, when we read the Scriptures, we can see there is much more. We can see God has a plan for us (Jeremiah 29:11, Ephesians 2:10). We can see that God gave us the place of authority with Him (Ephesians 2:6). We can see that God has given us the authority to bind and loose (Matthew 18:18). We can see that He wants us to live an abundant life (John 10:10). We can see that He expects us to be a blessing.

These are just a few of the incredible truths in the Word about you and me. To have what God has prom-ised, to do what God has said, we must go to the next step: changing the way we think. When I was younger, I was taught to go to church. I was taught to respect the church. I thought that was all God wanted. I didn't understand that I was created in God's image and likeness. I didn't understand that I was a spirit being, who possesses a soul and live in a body.

I wasn't taught, to bring the Word home and meditate it. I wasn't taught to renew my mind. I didn't know I needed to renew my mind. I didn't understand the power in renewing the mind.

But, as I said earlier, God has a way of getting you on track to walk in His perfect will. When I began to understand that being born again is major; but the next step of renewing my mind, was just as major, I started the process.

In Romans 12:2, the Holy Spirit had Paul write a message, which needs to echoed in the lives of every believer.

> And be not conformed to this world: but be ye transformed by the renewing of your mind, that ye may prove what *is* that good, and acceptable, and perfect, will of God. Romans 12:2 KJV

I believe this truth will move us from being faithful church members to being an example of Jesus here on this earth. We will see the church as not just four walls. But, we will see ourselves the way God does, we will see ourselves doing those things God has commanded. We will be the salt of the earth. We will be the light that God has said we would be. We will possess what God has said we could have. We will be an example of love as Jesus was.

Moving from a church member to a true disciple of Christ, starts with changing the way you think. To grow and develop spiritually, you must renew your minds to the Word of God. If you will enter into the mind renewal process, it will revolutionize your life and you will be more of a blessing to others.

Ephesians 4:23–24 says, "And be renewed in the spirit of your mind; And that ye put on the new man, which after God is created in righteousness and true holiness."

Another reason mind renewal is important is: we all have thoughts that do not agree with God's will. So we must exchange our thoughts for God's thoughts. And, finally, we know there is an enemy who attacks us in our mind. To demolish those thoughts, we must enter into the mind renewal process. Failure to enter into the mind renewal process, will leave us at a state of complacency, of average. And, we will only touch the surface of what God has for us to do and to receive.

Remember, the Bible mentioned 3 minds: the natural mind, the carnal mind and the spiritual (renewed) mind. Being saved is vital. By being saved, we are redeemed from the second death. We are redeemed from eternal damnation.

When we renew our minds, we live out the life Jesus purchased and planned for us. Remember, Jesus and the Word are one. When we go to church, we do fellowship with the Word and with each other. But, I want you to understand, that you should not stop there. There is more! We must take that preached Word home and renovate our minds to it. When you renovate something, it takes, discipline, patience and consistency.

Our lives will go in the direction of our thinking. Therefore, our thinking is important. I want to go the way of God all the days of my life. Don't you? If you do, start with the processing of changing your thinking. Start meditating the Word, confessing the Word, and acting on the Word. Let's take our time and read our text scripture, Romans 12:2,

> Do not be conformed to this world (this age), [fashioned after and adapted to its external, superficial customs], but be transformed (changed) by the [entire] renewal of your mind [by its new ideals and its new attitude], so that you may prove [for yourselves] what is the good and acceptable and perfect will of God, even the thing which is good and acceptable and perfect [in His sight for you]. (AMPC)

Then [in the final time] I will give you [spiritual] shepherds after My own heart, who will feed you with knowledge and [true] understanding."

~ Jeremiah 3:15 AMP

We are in the final times. God spoke these words thousands of years ago, looking forward to the twenty first century. He saw the final times and He said He wanted to provide pastors after His own heart for His blood bought church.

The word "feed" here implies "to teach". The pastors are God's gift to the body of Christ to teach His children His Word.

For every one that useth milk is unskilful in the word of righteousness: for he is a babe.

~ Hebrews 5:13 KJV

The writer of Hebrews says a babe is unskilled in the Word. A person who has attended church faithfully for twenty-five years and has not renewed his mind is considered a babe. No one should be in church for twenty-five years and still be a babe.

As newborn babes, desire the sincere milk of the word that ye may grow thereby.

~ 1 Peter 2:2 KJV

The Word does not come in milk form. It takes a person who is skillful in the Word and led by the Holy Spirit to pull the milk out so we can grow. In most cases, it is the pastor. The pastor will first lay the foundation of the Word and then we must receive it and meditate on it. As we study the Word, the Holy Spirit will minister to us. Remember, how Joshua meditated the Word. The more He meditated the Word, the image of that Word became real to Him. We must receive the preached Word as if it is God speaking directly to us. I Thessalonians reads,

> That ye would walk worthy of God, who hath called you unto his kingdom and glory. For this cause also thank we God without ceasing, because, when ye received the word of God which ye heard of us, ye received it not as the word of men, but as it is in truth, the word of God, which effectually worketh also in you that believe.

> ~ 1 Thessalonians 2:12–13 KJV

The preached Word has the power to save our souls!

> And he gave some, apostles; and some, prophets; and some, evangelists; and some, pastors and teachers;

> ~ Ephesians 4:11 KJV

Men are anointed by the Holy Spirit to speak the will of God. They are gifts from God. They are not God; but His vessels.

Let's look at 1 Peter 5:

> Therefore, I strongly urge the elders among you [pastors, spiritual leaders of the church], as a fellow elder and as an eyewitness [called to testify] of the sufferings of Christ, as well as one who shares in the glory that is to be revealed: shepherd *and* guide *and* protect the flock of God among you, exercising oversight not under compulsion, but voluntarily, according to *the will of* God; and not [motivated] for shameful gain, but with wholehearted enthusiasm; not lording it over those assigned to your care [do not be arrogant or overbearing], but be examples [of Christian living] to the flock [set a pattern of integrity for your congregation].
>
> ~ 1 Peter 5:1–3 AMP

Based on these Scriptures how can you grow if you neglect the leadership that God has placed over you? Your ministry gift, your Pastor, is one of the most critical components to helping you change your way of thinking. As we receive the preached Word, we can renew our minds to it (Mark 4:24).

The mind is the place where thoughts come that oppose the will of God. Webster 1828 dictionary defines oppose as to resist, to act against. If those thoughts are left unchecked, your life will be chaotic. If your life is chaotic, the door to enemy has been left open. Close it by meditating, confessing and acting on the Word. The life God has promised us is available. The tool He uses is His Word. If you are willing to put forth the effort and self-discipline to renovate your thinking, which was formed by your environment, associations and experiences, your life will soar. And, the words of Jesus in John 10:10 (AMP) will be a reality to you:

> **10** The thief comes only in order to steal and kill and destroy. *I came that they may have and enjoy life, and have it in abundance [to the full, till it overflows].*

I pray that you are ready to go to the next level in Christ. We are in the end times. When you look around us, there is chaos everywhere. So many blame God. But, He is not the blame; He is the Healer! He is the Provider! He is Love!

God, Jesus, the Holy Spirit and the heroes of faith who have gone on before us, are cheering us on! Even the earth is groaning to see us stand in our place. Romans 8:19 (AMPC) says,

For [even the whole] creation (all nature) waits expectantly and longs earnestly for God's sons to be made known [waits for the revealing, the disclosing of their sonship].

God wants us ready to stand in our authority, ready to take our place with full confidence knowing that what He has promised is sure. God is ready for us to be His hands, feet, eyes and mouth. But, it will take us growing up spiritually through the mind renewal process. He has put His faith in us that we will answer the call. The question is: Will you renew your mind? Will you change your thinking by meditation of the Word? I believe you are ready and willing to start this important process. So make this confession of faith:

Father, I thank You for the truth concerning mind renewal. With the help of the Holy Spirit, I will meditate, study, confess and act on Your Word on a daily basis. I believe that as my mind is being renewed, I will be able to stand in the authority of Christ and do all that You have purposed me to do and have all that You have purchased for Me. My life will go in the direction of Your Word, in Jesus Name.

Notes

_____

_____

_____

_____

_____

_____

_____

_____

_____

_____

_____

Prayer of Salvation

Scriptures (John 3:15–17,
Romans 10:9–10, Galatians 3:26,
2 Corinthians 5:17, 2 Corinthians 5:21)

Lord God, I come today to take You at your Word.
I do believe in my heart that Jesus Christ is Your Son.
I believe He died, was buried
and is now risen from the dead.
I believe He paid the price for sin for me.
Jesus, I receive You as my Savior and my Lord.
Come into my heart right now.

I believe I am a child of God.
I am born again. I am redeemed.
I am a new creation in Christ Jesus;
old things have passed away
and I have a new beginning.
Holy Spirit, help me to live this new life
I now have, in Jesus Name.

I thank You Father.
Amen.

Biography

Dr. A. L. Richardson Sr. is the Senior Pastor of Christian Life Bible Church in Gretna and Baton Rouge La. He attended the University of New Orleans and served in the military during the Vietnam war. Through practical teaching and under the power of the Holy Spirit, he brings the life changing Word so God's people can know who they are in Christ, what they possess in Christ and what they can do through Christ. The mission and call is that of spiritual growth and development.

He was licensed and ordained by Dr. Doyle Buddy Harrison of Tulsa, OK. He is also the founder of the Men of Valor Elite Ministry (M.O.V.E.) and the Fellowship of Churches United Support (F.O.C.U.S.) where he serves as a mentor to Pastors. Dr. Richardson and his wife, Dr. Ava M. Richardson (co-pastor) are the proud parents of seven children.

www.ingramcontent.com/pod-product-compliance
Lightning Source LLC
LaVergne TN
LVHW021518080426
835509LV00018B/2556